Acoustic Maintenance: A Complete Do-It-Yourself Guide

By: Gayle Monroe

Copyright Gayle Monroe 2012. All rights reserved

No part of this publication may be reproduced, stored in retrieval system, copied in any form or by any means, electronic, mechanical, photocopying, recording or otherwise transmitted without written permission from the author. You must not circulate this book in any format. The opinions expressed in this book are solely the opinions of the author. The author represents and warrents that s/he either owns or has the legal right to publish all material in this book.

CONTENTS

INTRODUCTION 5

HOW A GUITAR WORKS 7

    The Headstock 9

    Tuning Machines 9

    Nut 9

    Neck 9

    Body 9

    Soundhole 10

    Braces Inside the Guitar 10

    Saddle 10

    The Bridge 10

    Frets 11

    Strings 11

THE IMPORTANCE OF HUMIDITY 12

    Controlling Humidity 14

    How to Make a Homemade Humidifier 14

GENERAL MAINTENANCE AND SET-UP 16

REMOVING THE STRINGS 19

CLEANING THE FRETBOARD 22

BRIDGE REPAIR 26

    GLUE THE BRIDGE 33

    WHAT IS A CAUL? 33

    GLUING THE BRIDGE 36

HARDWARE INSPECTION AND ADJUSTMENTS 38

INSTALLING NEW STRINGS 40

    Acoustic Guitar String Basics 40

    Strings for the 12 String Guitar 44

INSTALLING STRINGS ON A CLASSICAL GUITAR 45

INSTALLING STRINGS ON AN ACOUSTIC GUITAR 50

INSTALLING STRINGS ON A 12 STRING GUITAR 55

HOW TO USE A DIGITAL TUNER 58

TUNING WITHOUT A TUNER 59

TUNING A 12 STRING 62

ADJUSTING THE NECK OR TRUSS ROD 63

ADJUSTING THE ACTION 69

ADJUSTING THE SADDLE HEIGHT 70

ADJUSTING THE NUT HEIGHT 73

REMOVING THE NUT 73

ADJUSTING THE NUT SLOTS 74

ADJUSTING THE INTONATION 75

FINAL CHECK 78

PURCHASING A GUITAR 79

BUYING A NEW GUITAR 82

SETTING UP A BRAND NEW GUITAR 83

OTHER HARDWARE ADJUSTMENTS 85

FINAL WORDS 91

ABOUT THE AUTHOR: 92

CLEANING THE FRETBOARD 22

BRIDGE REPAIR 26

    GLUE THE BRIDGE 33

    WHAT IS A CAUL? 33

    GLUING THE BRIDGE 36

HARDWARE INSPECTION AND ADJUSTMENTS 38

INSTALLING NEW STRINGS 40

    Acoustic Guitar String Basics 40

    Strings for the 12 String Guitar 44

INSTALLING STRINGS ON A CLASSICAL GUITAR 45

INSTALLING STRINGS ON AN ACOUSTIC GUITAR 50

INSTALLING STRINGS ON A 12 STRING GUITAR 55

HOW TO USE A DIGITAL TUNER 58

TUNING WITHOUT A TUNER 59

TUNING A 12 STRING 62

ADJUSTING THE NECK OR TRUSS ROD 63

ADJUSTING THE ACTION 69

ADJUSTING THE SADDLE HEIGHT 70

ADJUSTING THE NUT HEIGHT 73

REMOVING THE NUT 73

ADJUSTING THE NUT SLOTS 74

ADJUSTING THE INTONATION 75

FINAL CHECK 78

PURCHASING A GUITAR 79

BUYING A NEW GUITAR 82

SETTING UP A BRAND NEW GUITAR 83

OTHER HARDWARE ADJUSTMENTS 85

FINAL WORDS 91

ABOUT THE AUTHOR: 92

Introduction

Acoustic guitars have been providing musical entertainment for hundreds of years and continue to be one of the most popular instruments played by thousands of professional and amateur musicians all over the world.

Acoustic guitars come in a large variety of styles and you can purchase one that fits your musical taste and playing style. The most common types are the 6 string guitar with steel strings; the classical guitar, a 6 string with nylon strings; and the 12 string guitar which usually has steel strings as well.

New guitars, at least those that are not antiques or collectors items, come in prices ranging from under $150 on up and you can easily find a used guitar for under $100 in decent playing condition. This is one reason why they are so popular; they are affordable and portable. You can take a guitar just about anywhere and you don't need to plug it in, so it's perfect for camping, the beach, or taking to a friends house for a jam session. Now, if you've invested $1,000 or more on your guitar, taking it camping is probably not a good idea, which is one of the reasons why most serious guitar players own more than one instrument.

Acoustic guitars are living, breathing instruments. Not literally, of course, but even after the tree has been cut and the guitar has been crafted from its wood, it is still alive, changing with the climate and environment. This is important to understand as the environment in which your guitar lives will affect its playability and its quality over the years. A guitar that is well maintained will retain its value and will evolve into a smooth, mellow instrument. You will find that a new guitar purchased today, if taken care of, will sound even more beautiful 20 years down the road.

Although many repair jobs for an acoustic guitar should be left to the capable hands of a skilled luthier, there are many basic maintenance and repair jobs that you, as a guitar owner, can do yourself if you take the time to do them right. Simple tasks such as cleaning, changing strings and adjusting the neck can be done with simple tools and supplies. Other maintenance procedures, such as adjusting the intonation or action, are a bit more complicated but can easily be done yourself using tools found at home or in most hardware stores. You can even go further to say that repair jobs such as nut or bridge replacements can be done at home as long as certain procedures are followed carefully.

It takes patience to do repair work on a guitar. This purpose of this book is to show you the steps necessary to do regular maintenance and basic repairs on your acoustic guitars. It will show you how to:

- Clean your guitar
- Change the strings
- Tune your guitar
- Adjust the truss rod
- Adjust the nut height
- Adjust the saddle height

You will learn how to set the action to match your playing style. You will also learn how to replace the nut or saddle and how to remove and re-glue the bridge.

This book will cover these steps using three different guitar styles. The six string guitar, the classical guitar, and the 12 string guitar. The guitars used in this book are a new Taylor 215ce. These are very nice middle of the road guitars. Taylor guitars are built on a mass scale but with attention to quality and detail which results in a beautiful, bright sounding instrument.

The classical guitar used in this book is a La Patric, made in Canada. This was a beautiful sounding instrument that had a unfortunate accident with a flying shoe (one of the hazards of leaving your guitar on display in an active living area) resulting in a long crack on the top and the bridge became lifting from the top as well. In this book you will witness an attempt to bring it back to, at a minimum, a playable level.

Finally, the 12 string in this book is a Yamaha APX700 II. Yamaha makes a good quality and very affordable guitar. It is the opinion of this author that yamaha guitars give you a lot of bang for the buck. You can pick up a very nice sounding yamaha for a couple hundred dollars and they make great beginner guitars. Of course, selecting a guitar brand is a personal choice and one should select a guitar based on how it feels to each individual player.

How a Guitar Works

The first and most basic step in doing your own maintenance and repairs on your guitar is to understand how a guitar works. How does a wooden box with strings produce not just sound, but perfectly tuned sound?

Sound, as you may already know is simply a bunch of vibrations that the human brain translates into something recognizable such as speech, a dog barking, a bird chirping, a car engine, a siren, etc. With a guitar, the strings vibrate in a certain way to make a recognizable sound. More specifically, it makes a tone. A tone is a single sound wave at a certain frequency. This is different from sound or random noise which is a mixture of many frequencies at varied volumes. So, it is more accurate to say that a guitar produces tones, rather than just sound. These tones are put together in a way that is pleasing to the human brain producing what we call, music. A musical note is a tone and chord, such as one played on a guitar, is a group of tones that compliment each other creating a pleasing sound.

Guitars produce these tones using vibrating strings that resonate throughout a wooden box, so to speak. Actually, it's a little more complicated than that but not too much. Without getting too much into music theory, let's look at what produces a perfectly tuned tone on a guitar. To do this, we will first talk about the parts of the guitar and the role they play in producing a tone.

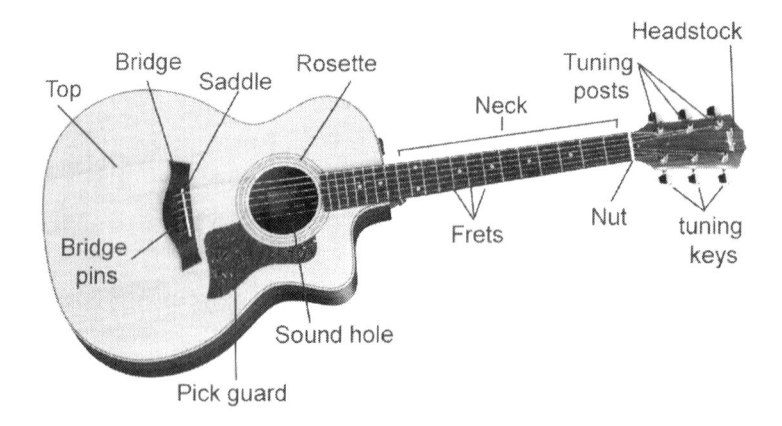

The Headstock
The headstock is where the tuning machines are attached, which is its main purpose in life.

Tuning Machines
The tuning machines consist of the tuning post, the tuning keys and the mechanisms to make them turn

Nut
The nut is the piece of bone or synthetic material that attaches at the top of the fretboard. The purpose of the nut is to stop the vibration of the strings at a certain point. You will notice that the strings will suddenly bend downward at the nut. This is a very important part of the guitar when producing a tone.

Neck
The neck is made of a solid block of wood and in most guitars, with the exception of some classical guitars, a steel rod travels down the center of the neck. This rod, called the truss rod, is responsible for holding the neck flat and in one piece under the pressure of the strings. Without it, the neck of the guitar would bend forward when the strings are tightened and certainly break under the pressure. The truss rod can be adjusted allowing you to control how much bow is in the neck. This adjustment will affect the pitch of the strings but is not really responsible for producing the sound.

Body
The body of the guitar is made from different types of woods. The body is precisely shaped, crafted and glued in a manner that produces the most pleasing tones possible. The top of the guitar is the main part of the body that produces sound. It is made of softer more springy woods such a spruce so that it can vibrate when the strings are plucked or strummed. The guitar sides vibrate much less and the back doesn't vibrate at all due to the fact that it's

resting against the guitar player preventing vibration.

Soundhole

The soundhole is the large round hole on the top of the guitar. This allows the air that is resinating through the guitar body allowing the sound to escape so your audience can hear it. Guitar designers will sometimes experiment with different soundhole shapes. Modern guitars will place the soundhole in different areas on the guitar body which actually changes its overall sound. Some hollow body guitars will have f holes cut in the top which help in projecting the sounds. It is more common to see f holes in guitars that have some type of electronic pickups to aid in the volume and sound of the guitar.

Braces Inside the Guitar

The guitar body includes braces that are glued to the guitar top on the inside. These braces help control the amount of vibration in the wood. For example, when sound waves pass through the soundhole it causes the the edges of the soundhole to vibrate and, if it vibrates too much, it could produce noise, rather than a tone. Braces around the soundhole will control the amount of vibration so the guitar produces the tones you're looking for.

Saddle

The saddle is similar to the nut. It is made of a long, thin piece of bone or synthetic material and is placed at the bridge. It's purpose is to stop the vibration of the strings at a certain point.

The Bridge

The bridge is responsible for transferring the vibration of the strings to the top of the guitar. The amount of energy put into the strings, or how hard you pluck or strum, directly transfers into the bridge and into the guitar body. Therefore, the bridge plays an important role in producing music.

Frets

Frets are the thin metal strips that run across the neck. This purpose of a fret is to stop the vibration of the strings wherever you place your fingers. Sounds a lot like the saddle and the nut, right?

Strings

That takes us to the most important part of how a guitar works, the strings. Tones of a guitar are effected by four variables:

- String length
- Strings tension
- String thickness
- String elasticity, or springiness

The length of a string changes the frequency of the string, the longer the string, the lower the frequency. The shorter the string, the higher the frequency. Remember, tones are different frequencies that our ears hear and our brain interprets as pitch, or how high or low the sound is.

The pitch of a guitar string is controlled by its length. Have you ever notice how bass guitars have much longer strings and guitars, ukuleles and mandolins have much shorter strings? The string length is controlled by the nut and saddle. The length of the string between the nut and the saddle is called its vibrating length. The vibrating length of a typical acoustic guitar is between 24 and 26 inches. You can change the length of the strings by pressing down on the neck at a certain fret causing the string to shorten, therefore causing its frequency to be higher.

The second factor is string tension. The tighter you wind a string, the higher its tone. You can experiment with a rubber band to see just how this works. Of course, you can only stretch a string so far before it breaks. The high E string is under a lot more tension than the low E string.

The third factor is string thickness. Thicker strings vibrate more slowly which results in a lower tone. Thinner strings vibrate faster, producing a higher tone.

Lastly, is the string's elasticity. The materials used to make a guitar string will affect the speed at which it vibrates. Different guitars, such as classical guitars or electric guitars, will use strings made of different types of materials, which will produce a more brassy tone or a full tone.

All of these factors together will produce the desired tone for each string of your guitar. Understanding these concepts will help you troubleshoot any problems that you may have with your guitar. If the intonation is off, or if you are hearing a buzzing sound, you will have a better understanding of why and of how to fix it.

The Importance of Humidity

Relative humidity is simply the amount of moisture that is in the air. The higher the humidity, the more water vapor there is floating through the atmosphere. The lower the humidity, the less water vapor. Wood expands and contracts with humidity conditions. It swells when the humidity is high and shrinks when it is low.

One of the most important things you can do to take care of your acoustic guitar is to keep its humidity at a controlled level. Wood will react to the surrounding environment and, during the winter months when the heater or furnace is on, your guitar can suffer due to the dry air. If you've ever walked into a good guitar store and notice an enclosed room where the acoustic guitars are displayed, this room will usually be humidity controlled. You'll notice it when you walk in. The ideal humidity for an acoustic guitar is right around 40% to 50%. However, the typical home in dry climates or when the heater is on in winter months, the humidity is much lower than 50%.

If your guitar becomes too dry, it will begin to develop some very serious problems such as the bridge lifting away from the body, cracks in the wood, frets extending from the sides of the fretboard. These are extreme problems that result from a guitar being constantly neglected as far as humidity, but there are more subtle signs to watch for.

When wood dries it shrinks and there are certain places where your guitar will show signs of shrinking. Looking at the guitar top, just behind the bridge, a dry guitar will begin to sink down in this area and the bridge will begin to lift the body up causing a wavy look to the wood. If you cant see it by looking at it, just put a straight edge on the top of the guitar. In severe cases the bridge will begin to lift from the guitar from the pressure of the strings.

A guitar can also develop cracks at the seams. Where the top and back connect to the sides of the guitar, a crack may develop if the guitar is too dry. Some guitar backs will be two pieces of wood glued at the center. A crack may appear at the seam if the guitar is too dry. Another problem that is a sure sign are frets that extend beyond the fretboard. This happens because the wood of the fretboard shrinks. You may also start to hear your strings buzzing on the frets because, as the guitar shrinks, the action will lower.

Lack of humidity can destroy a guitar. It's something that a lot of guitar owners forget about or neglect, but it is a very important component to good guitar maintenance. But, in addition to your guitar becoming too dry, your guitar can also become too moist if you live in a very humid climate. High humidity can cause the action to go up, it can cause glue joints to fail and can cause the bridge to pop up. There are humidifiers on the market that will not only provide moisture for your guitar, but will also absorb it if the climate is too humid.

Controlling Humidity

Controlling your guitar's humidity is easy to do. There are a number of humidifiers available on the market that are inexpensive and easy to use. Some humidifiers fit directly into the sound hole of your guitar and come with a seal so that the moisture stays inside the guitar. Other sound hole humidifiers simply hang down from the strings inside the sound hole. You can also place humidifiers in your guitar case to control the humidity. You can even purchase hard shell cases with humidifiers built in.

Humidifiers consist of a couple of basic components: a sponge and a perforated container to hold the moist sponge while allowing the moisture to escape. Many will also come with a way to attach themselves to the guitar. Because of the simple and basic design, there is no reason why you can't make your own humidifier out of basic household items.

How to Make a Homemade Humidifier

Here's how to make a simply humidifier that you can keep inside your guitar case

Materials needed:

- A plastic container such as a soap dish with a lid, a small plastic food container with a lid or a pill bottle.
- Common household kitchen sponge
- A drill or Dremel to make the holes

Six Steps to a Homemade Humidifier:
1. With your drill or Dremel, carefully drill holes into the top, sides and bottom of the plastic container. The holes should be about a quarter of an inch apart. The amount of holes will depend on the size of the container. You could drill 24 holes if they will fit.
2. Clean away any plastic pieces left over from drilling
3. Cut the sponges so they fit snugly into the container
4. Wet the sponge with water and completely wring out the water. The sponge should be moist, not dripping wet.
5. Place the sponges in the container, put the lid on the container
6. Place your new humidifier into your guitar case

The important thing to remember when making your own humidifier or using a purchased humidifier is to never allow it to drip. You do not want water touching the wood of the guitar in any way.

To monitor the humidity of your guitar, you can purchase a low priced digital hydrometer to keep in your guitar case. That way, you will always know if your guitar is being stored at an acceptable level of humidity.

Before you begin doing setup adjustments you should make sure your guitar is at an acceptable humidity level. If your guitar is dry, use a humidifier and store it in its case. Check the moisture of the sponge each day and also check the condition of the guitar. Once it is at the proper level, which may take several days, you can move on to the rest of the setup and maintenance procedures.

General Maintenance and Set-Up

Every guitar needs tender loving care in the form of basic maintenance and an occasional setup. If you play on a regular basis, once a day or every other day, it's a good idea to do thorough maintenance on your guitar 2 or 3 times a year. Each time you change the strings you should be inspecting all the areas covered in a set up, although adjustments probably won't be necessary that often.

With a little practice, you can do a complete set up in about an hour or two depending on how much adjustment your guitar needs. Each time you do maintenance on your guitar do so with a lot of patience and careful adjustments. Never rush the process or you could cause more damage.

The steps in guitar maintenance should be done in a specific order as one adjustment will effect the adjustment following. Below is a list of steps to take when doing a complete setup on your guitar. This book will talk about each step of the process in detail.

Steps of the Maintenance Procedure
1. Remove the strings

2. Clean the surface of the guitar

3. Clean the fretboard

4. Check the bridge
5. Check the headstock and tuning machines
6. Install new strings
7. Adjust truss rod
8. Adjust nut
9. Adjust bridge saddle for intonation

Materials Needed

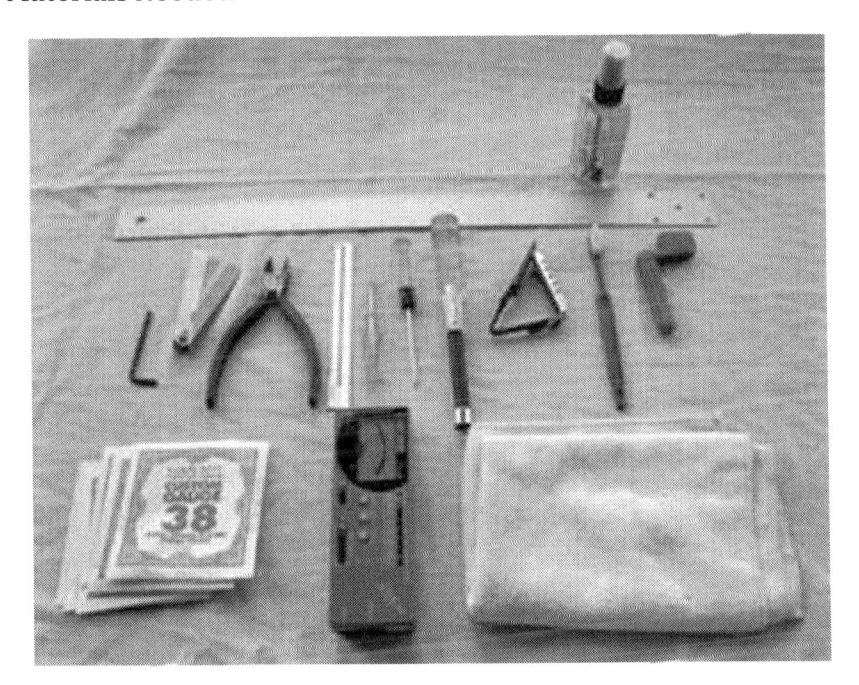

- 12" or 18" metal ruler
- Allen wrench or truss rod tool
- Wire cutters
- small philips screwdriver

- small standard screwdriver
- wrench to fit the tuning key nuts
- capo
- string winder
- new strings
- tuner
- clean polishing rag
- fretboard oil

Removing the Strings

Removing guitar strings is a quick and easy process. Start by unwinding the strings at the tuning posts. Using a string winder will make this process much faster.

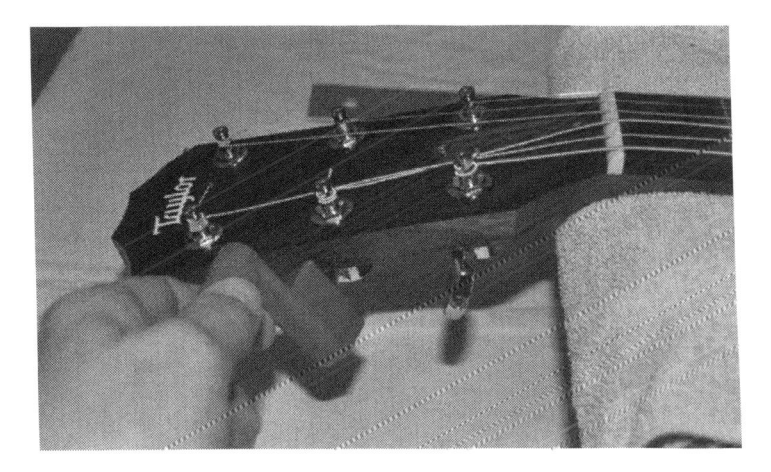

At this point you can remove the pins from the bridge. String winders will come with a round notch at one end. This is a tool for removing the bridge pins. Before you use it, be sure to place something soft under the winder so it doesn't damage the bridge surface when you pry out the bridge pin.

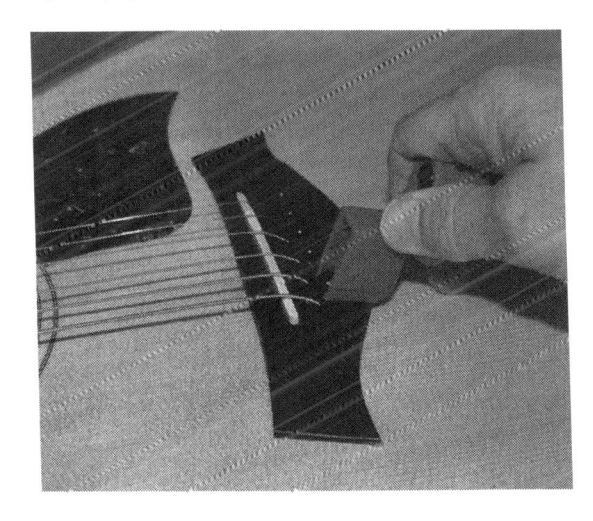

Sometimes the pins can be stubborn and the winder doesn't provide enough force. If this is the case, you can use wire cutters to gently lift them from the bridge.

Some people like to cut the strings before removing them. It's not necessary, but it does make it easier to remove strings from classical guitars or any type of guitar where the string has to slide through a hole in the bridge. In the case of a guitar with bridge pins, it does nothing to make the job easier. But if you do cut the strings, always make sure you unwind the strings beforehand so there is no sudden release of tension on the neck or a string flying into you.

Cleaning Your Guitar

The surface of most acoustic guitars will have a finish that requires a very light coating of wax. The wax will help prevent small scratches. A very good cleaner for any lacquer finish on a guitar is a basic, automotive clear wax. Turtle wax and McGuire's both make a clear wax polish that will work on your guitar. This cleaning product will remove dust, dirt and oils from the surface of the guitar. It will also buff out any light scratches and add a protective coating. Plus, it make your guitar beautiful and shiny. One thing you do not want to use is a product with a silicone base such as those used on your car's interior. Silicone based products will sometimes have a bad reaction with the finish.

Spray a small amount of cleaner on to a clean polishing rag and and clean the entire surface of the guitar except for those areas with bare wood, such as the fretboard. Don't forget to apply the polish to the back of the neck. This is where a lot of gunk can build up from your hands while playing. Cleaning it will actually help speed up your playing. Flip the rag over to a dry area and give the surface a good polish.

If your guitar has a satin finish, don't use any type of cleaning polish or wax based cleaners. The best solution for cleaning a satin finish is to use a clean cloth and warm water. For areas that have stubborn dirt you can use a very small amount of mild soap, then wipe it with a clean damp cloth.

This cleaning step is a good time to do a thorough inspection of the guitar surface, the glue joints on all the sides of the guitar and where the neck attaches. Look for any small cracks that might indicate a dry guitar that requires a humidifier.

Cleaning the Fretboard

As you play your guitar, oils and dirt from your fingers will build up on the frets. Each time you change your strings or do a guitar set up, you should clean the fretboard. There are a couple of ways to do this.

Method 1
The first method is to clean the fretboard with fine steel wool. Use a grade 0000 (sometimes called four zero) steel wool. This is not the steel wool that you use to clean your dirty pots and pans. This grade is much finer and is pure steel wool, with no soaps or added cleaners. It is available at most hardware stores.

NOTE: For acoustic/electric guitars using magnetic pickups, cover the sound hole with some tape before proceeding. Magnetic pickups can attract the small particles of steel and may cause trouble with your electronics. Covering the sound hole is a simple way to protect your guitar's electronics.

With a small piece, lightly rub the steel wool in the direction of of the wood grain to sand off the dirt and grime. You will notice that a lot of dirt will build up directly along side of the metal frets. You can use an object with a sharp edge to scrape this out but be careful not to apply any pressure so you don't scratch the surface of the fretboard. You can also use the steel wool on the surface of the frets to remove any tarnish or oxidation.

Using a soft, dry brush, such as a paint brush, remove the loose dirt and steel wool particles from the fretboard and from the top surface of the guitar. Use a clean cloth to rub down the fretboard to get rid of any remaining dust and dirt.

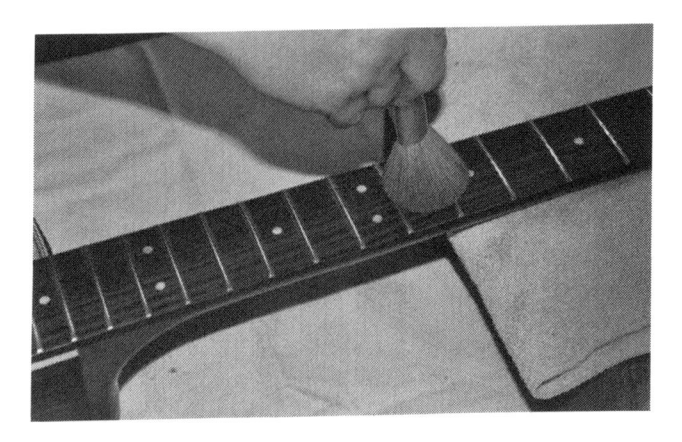

The next step is to apply a small amount of oil to the fretboard. Most guitar shops will sell a product specifically designed for this purpose. Place a small amount of oil on a clean paper towel or rag and apply a thin layer of oil along the entire fretboard. Do not saturate the wood with a lot of oil. Work the oil into the wood with the rag then, using a dry paper towel, wipe away any excess oils from the fretboard. The purpose of this is to keep the bare wood conditioned which will make it last longer and prevent damage to the fretboard. It will also help keep the fretboard clean. The oils will repel dirt from your hands making it easier to clean off using the method just described.

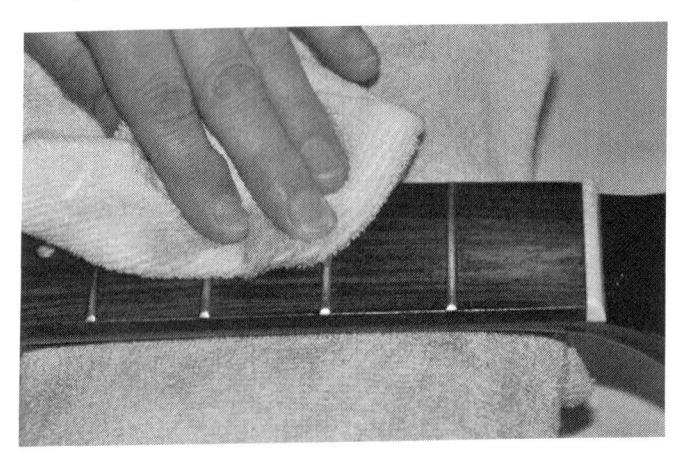

Method 2

The second method is to use the fretboard oil as a cleaning product along with a very soft toothbrush. Apply a small amount of fretboard oil and use the toothbrush to gently scrub away any dirt and grime. Use very light pressure and be sure to work the brush along the edges of the frets to remove the buildup of dirt.

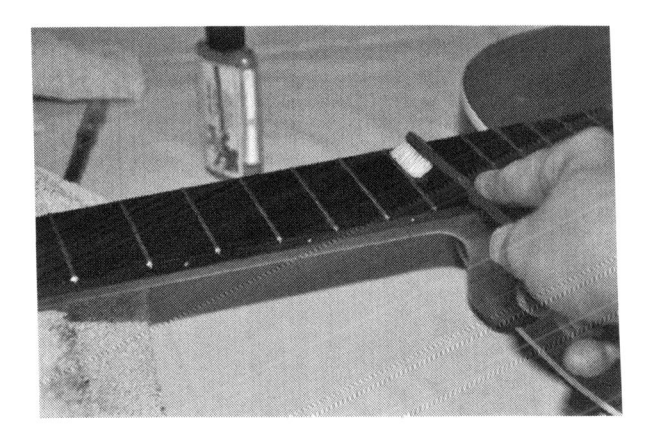

Use a clean dry cloth or paper towel to remove any excess oil and dirt. It's a good idea to go over this area several times with a new, dry towel. Using the fretboard oil to clean with will usually require more oil so you want to make sure you wipe away all of it and give the fretboard a good polish.

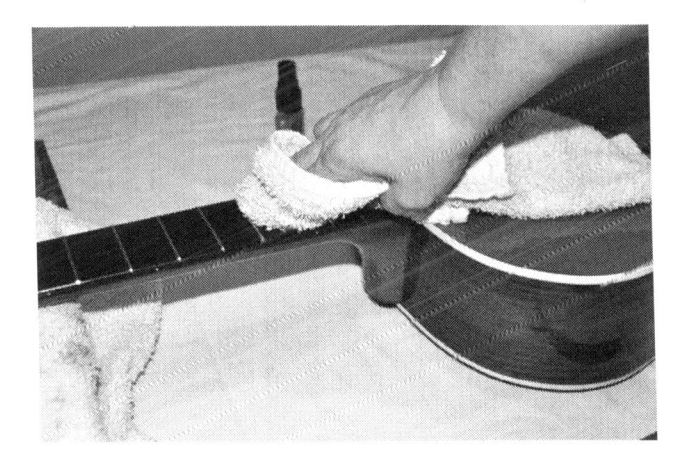

Bridge Repair

This topic may seem a bit out of order. What is a major repair job doing in the set up section? But, if you have a guitar with a bridge problem, you will need to fix the bridge before you can move on to any of the set up procedures.

As mentioned in the introduction, the classical guitar used in this book had an unfortunate accident. It was places on a stand in the front room of an active household and a shoe, which inadvertently flew off someone's foot, hit the front of the guitar causing a nasty crack in the wood. The guitar was not playable as the bridge had been lifted from the surface. A quick assessment at a local guitar repair shop priced the repair job at $300, more than half the price of the guitar itself. So the owner made an effort to fix the bridge, but, didn't follow proper procedures. The bridge itself was not broken or cracked but was coming loose. When this happens, one can not simply add glue under the bridge and allow it to dry. A proper fix requires removal of the bridge and removal of all the old glue before it can be replaced. Glue will not stick to old glue. Inevitably, the guitar owner was having trouble with broken strings, tuning problems and major intonation issues.

This section of the book will demonstrate how to re-glue the bridge properly. The method described will work for any flat top acoustic guitar either nylon string or steel string. Replacing or re-gluing the bridge is one of the more advanced repairs you can do to your guitar but it is possible to do it yourself at home without special tools. Follow the steps carefully and remember to work slowly. Rushing through this job will result in damage to the top of your guitar which is the one thing you absolutely want to avoid.

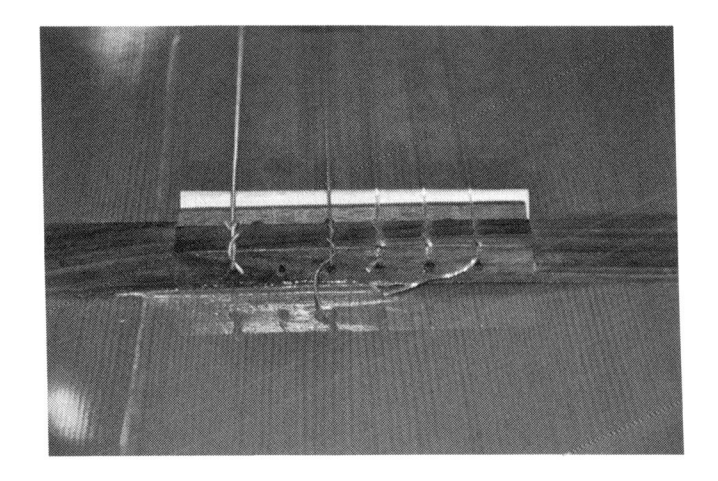

Before you perform this procedure on your own guitar, read through the process completely. Then you can determine if this is a project you want to do yourself or take it in to a technician.

Materials needed:

Hot iron

Hot water

Small paint brush

Thin spatula or putty knife

Razor blade or x-acto knife

Sand paper

A moist towel

Remove the Bridge

After removing the strings remove the saddle. On most acoustic guitars the saddle will simply lift out of the bridge. It should not be glued in place. Keep it in a safe place so it doesn't get lost or broken.

Mask off the bridge by applying painter's tape or non-tacky tape to the surface of the guitar around the bridge. This will protect the top of the guitar from getting scratched or damaged and will give you a reference point as to where the bridge should be place when ready to glue.

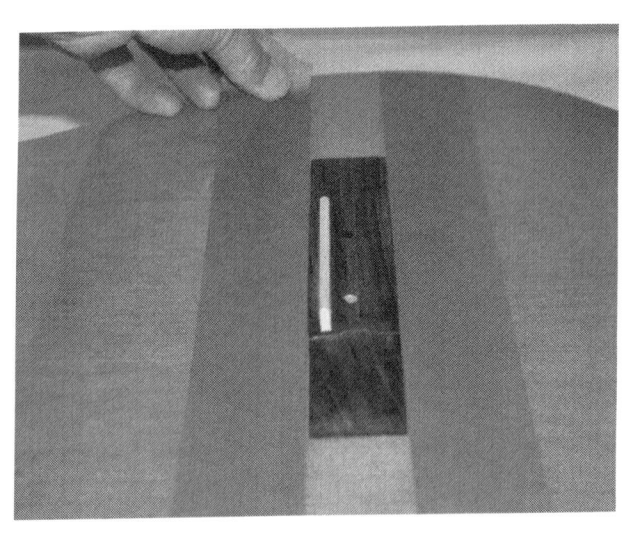

To remove the bridge without destroying the top of your guitar you will need to heat up the glue that holds the bridge on. Do not simply pry the bridge off using force. If you do this, you will take pieces of the guitar top off with it. You want to start off by heating up the glue to soften it so it will be easier to work a puddy knife under the bridge. Luthiers will sometimes use heaters that are specifically designed for this type of work, but it's not likely that the average guitar player is going to have this equipment handy. So, here's a trick to warming up the glue. Begin by laying a damp cloth on top of the bridge and place a hot iron on top of the towel. The steam from the towel to seep into the wood and warm up the glue.

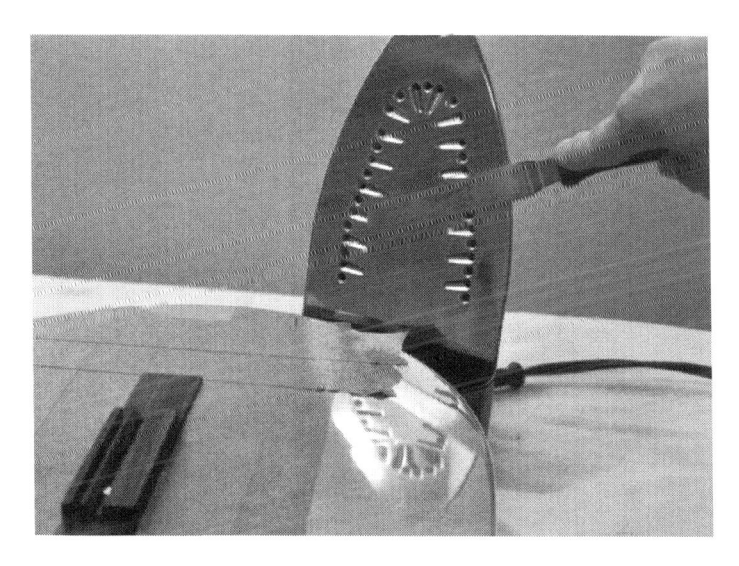

Next, heat up the tip of the putty knife using the iron. In this example I'm using a small kitchen spatula. It has a very thin flexible blade making it perfect for this job. You can also use a painters knife which also have a very thin blade.

Gently work the hot putty knife under the edges of the bridge. Use some pressure, but not too much. Work from the outside edges toward the middle of the bridge. As the heat from the putty knife works to warm up the glue, you will begin to feel the knife slip farther under the bridge. If you hear any cracking noises, back off a little. This means the glue may be pulling some wood splinters off the guitar. Continue to heat up the knife and gently work your way around the bridge.

This process will take about 20 minutes depending on how stubborn the bridge is. Some bridges will pop off rather easily and some, such as the one used in the example, will take a lot of patience. Continue heating the putty knife and working your way under the bridge until it easily comes off the surface of the guitar. A successful bridge removal means the bridge comes off in one piece, it does not have splinters of wood glued to it, and the surface of the guitar is left in tact.

In the example shown, the previous bridge repair job was done so poorly that it took a lot of work to soften the glue and, because the old glue was not removed before the new glue was applied, the wood splintered and a portion of the guitar top came loose when the bridge came off. When the bridge is re-glued properly, it should work fine, but now the guitar has some nasty cosmetic damage.

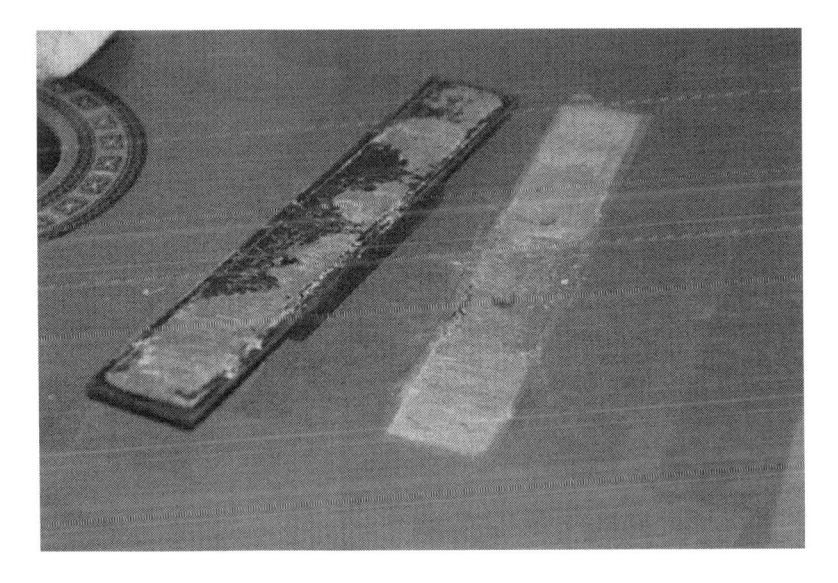

Now that the bridge is off the guitar, it's time to remove any remaining glue from both the guitar surface and the underside of the bridge. Using a razor blade, carefully scrape away the thin layer of glue that is left over. Be very careful not to remove any wood during the process. Scrape all the way to the edges where the bare wood meets the lacquer finish. If there is a thick layer of glue, as in our example, you can soften the glue further by applying hot water with a soft paint brush. Us a sharp chisel to remove the excess glue. Work in small increments being careful not to remove any of the wood.

Once you have the surface of the guitar clean, it's time to do the same with the bottom of the bridge. Again, using a razor blade, carefully scrape away the thin layer of glue. In the example, some wood splinters from the guitar surface came up with the bridge, so the glue was scraped away using some hot water and the chisel. Once all the glue is removed, let the wood dry. You can speed up this process by using the head of a blow dryer. Give the bottom of the bridge a gentle sanding to remove any rough spots or bits of wood.

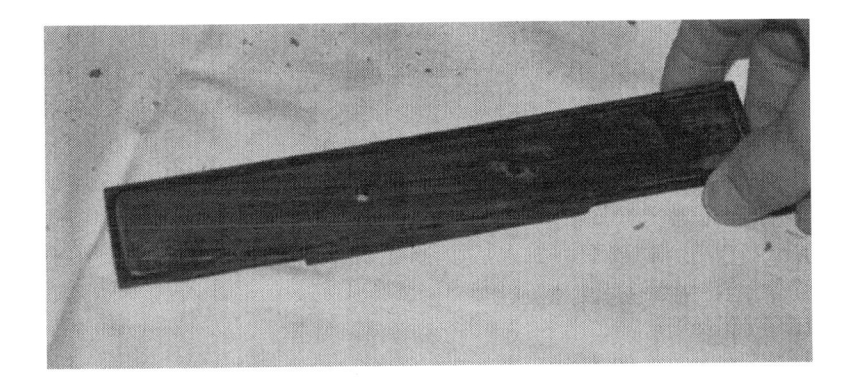

Glue the Bridge

Now that you have the surface of the guitar and the bridge ready to glue, you need to consider how you are going to apply the necessary pressure to the bridge to allow the glue to properly dry and cure. In order for the bridge to attache to the guitar evenly and to withstand the immense pressure exerted by the strings, the bridge needs to be properly clamped in place. The best way to do this is to invest in some woodworking clamps. six to eight inch C-Clamps work best for this type of situation. There are many other specialty clamps that are designed specifically for guitar bridges, but, if you don't plan on doing this kind of job very often, the you may want to think of other methods. Basically, you need to be able to apply constant and even pressure to the middle and the sides of the bridge while the glue is drying. This includes adding a caul inside the guitar to provide counter pressure. The clamps will press against the caul and the bridge and add the pressure without damaging the braces inside the guitar.

What is a Caul?

A caul is simply a block of wood that has been cut to fit the patterns of braces inside the guitar. Different guitars will have different brace patterns and luthiers and guitar technicians will have a collection of cauls to fit any guitar that's brought to them.

You may be able to find one for your specific guitar, but it is actually pretty easy to make one. Here's a sure fire method you can use to mad a caul for your guitar.

Materials for making a custom caul:

A 2x2 block of wood 6" or 7" long. Make sure you can fit it into the sound hole

A thin piece of styrofoam

Double sided tape

A saw

Using the double sided tape, place a layer of styrofoam on top of the block of wood. You can trim it to size so you don't have overhand.

Place the block into the sound hole and press the styrofoam side against the top of the guitar under the bridge. The braces will leave an imprint in the styrofoam. Remove the block and you will see exactly where you need to cut gaps for the braces.

Using a saw, cut along the indentations, cutting all the way into the wood. Remove the layer of styrofoam. Depending on how wide the braces are, you may have to cut thicker gaps into the block of wood. Keep checking the cut by placing the block into the guitar. The block of wood should have gaps in it that surround the braces and the block should set snugly against the underside of the guitar top. Now you have a caul custom made for your guitar.

The next thing you need to do before you glue the bridge is gather all the materials you will need to clamp down the bridge. The example shows a very low budget method for applying pressure to the bridge.

I've cut a 2x4 to fit inside the guitar wedged up against the underside of the bridge. This is not ideal because it is pressing against the braces and could potentially cause them to break loose from the guitar body. But in this case, considering the condition of the guitar, it should be worth the risk. To hold the bridge down I am using 20 pounds of weights with a bit of paper under to protect the surface of the bridge. To apply pressure. To the edges of the bridge I have cut two pieces of wooden dowels to fit just under the weights.

Before you apply any glue, do a dry run with your clamping system to make sure you can get everything set up before the glue dries. Once you you have it all figured out, you can move on to the glue. Make sure the masking tape is still applied to the surface of the guitar showing you the exact position where the bridge was before. If you don't place the bridge in the same spot, you will have some intonation problems. But as long as you have the masking tape down as a guide, it shouldn't be too difficult.

What Type of Glue?
There are two types of glue that work very well on wood instruments. The first is a glue that has been around for a long time and is made from the cellulose of animal hide. It's called hide glue. This glue, however is not for the beginner. It comes in powder form and must be mixed with water in the proper proportions.

Then it must be kept heated while being used. Hide glue dries very quickly and will start to gel as it dries. It is also very foul smelling.

The other type of glue is aliphatic resin glue, which is a common glue among woodworkers. This glue comes ready to use and is easy to apply with no special preparation. The most common brand among guitar technicians is Titebond although there are other brands of glue that will work fine for a guitar. This is the type of glue used in this bridge repair job.

Gluing the Bridge

Now that you have your clamps ready, or whatever mechanism you're going to use, and you have your glue ready, it's time to glue the bridge. Using a small paint brush, apply a thin layer of the glue to the surface of the guitar. Make sure you have the masking tape in place so you don't get glue on the surface of the guitar and so you have a reference on where to place the bridge.

Next, apply a coating of glue to the back of the bridge. Place the bridge on the top of the guitar aligning it carefully with the masking tape. Here's a little trick. Use a pair of chopsticks to alight the holes in the bridge to the holes in the guitar to for an exact fit. Choptsticks are perfect because they are tapered on the end and will fit any size hole depending on your guitar.

Place the clamps or weight onto the bridge and apply pressure. You will experience some squeeze out, or glue oozing around the edges of the bridge. You can see from the example shown that the 20 pounds of weight on the bridge with the block of wood underneath seems to be applying the necessary pressure.

Clean up the squeeze out with a damp, warm towel. This will also aid in getting the glue thoroughly into the joints. After cleaning up the squeeze out, let the guitar sit for 24 hours allowing the glue to dry and properly cure.

After 24 hours, remove the pressure from the bridge and check your work. If there is still some glue beyond the edges of the bridge, this can be cleaned up using some hot water applied with a paint brush. Use the heat to soften the glue and wipe it away with a cloth or scrape it away carefully with a razor blade. The bridge should now be securely glued to the guitar top and you should be ready to move on to the next steps; cleaning, and installing strings.

In looking at our repair job on the classical guitar, you can see that it is far from perfect. There are some cosmetic damages to the surface and the top of the guitar still has some wavy areas, although it is better than before the bridge was re-glued. The good news is that there is no damage to the braces inside the guitar and now the bridge is properly attached.

In assessing this repair job I've determined that it is worth the cost to invest in a few clamps. The method of balancing weights seems to work well enough but it seem very precarious and I was never quite sure if it was providing enough pressure in the right places. Clamps and a caul will take the guess work out of this job. Besides, if you only do this once, you can use the clamps for other jobs around the house, especially if you are into woodworking. I highly recommend purchasing clamps if you have a bridge repair in your future. We will be visiting this guitar as we move on with the setup procedures. Acoustic Guitar Strings

Hardware Inspection and Adjustments

All guitars come with various types of hardware, the main thing being the tuning machines found on the headstock. Over time the parts of the tuning machine can become loose causing your guitar to slip out of tune or causing buzzing or rattling noises when you play. Each time you change your strings you should always check for loose parts and tighten them if necessary.

Start by gently wiggling each tuning key by hand to see if it is loose. The knob should be slightly firm when you turn it but should not be difficult to turn. It should not spin freely.

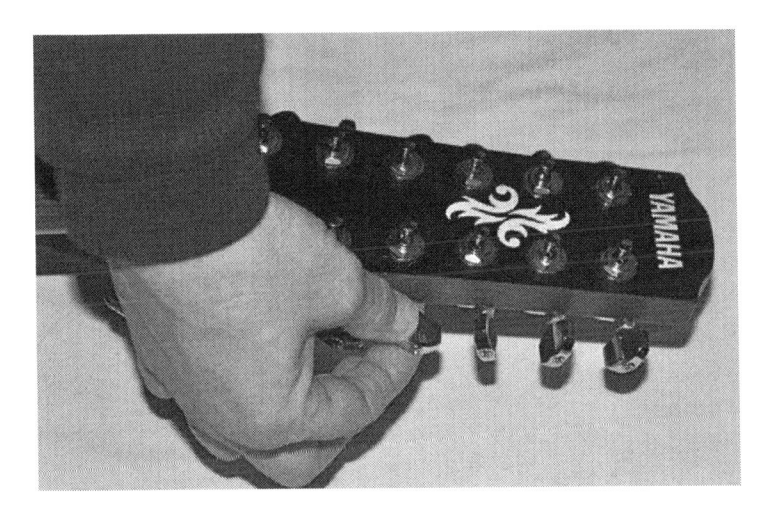

If it is loose, use a small screwdriver to tighten the small screw at the end of the tuning key. Turn it until the tuning key is tight but not difficult to turn.

Classical guitars have tuning pegs or posts that run through the wood of the headstock rather than sticking up as on other acoustic style guitars. These pegs are usually made of a type of hard plastic material or sometimes steel. Always inspect the pegs for cracks. If you find one that is cracked, it needs to be replaced. These often can only be purchased as a set. On most classical guitars three tuning pegs are attached together as part of a complete machine. Replacing the tuning machines is a fairly simple job. The next section shows how to do it on both the classical guitar and an acoustic guitar.

Installing New Strings

Now that you have the surface and fretboards clean, the tuning keys and machines cleaned and adjusted and any other hardware sufficiently tightened, it's time to install a new set of strings. All other adjustments done during the set up should be done with the neck under the tension of the strings brought up to standard pitch. This is done because the tension from the strings will cause the neck to bow, which is what you want, and this will allow you to get the proper adjustment on the neck, the saddle height and action.

Acoustic Guitar String Basics

The number one rule of guitar strings is change your strings and change them often. It's much easier to play new strings. They are much more flexible and easier to hold down, easier to bend, and they sound much better than dull, dirty, old strings.

How often should you change your strings? If you play your guitar every day, then you should change them every 2 months or maybe a little more often. If you don't play every day, then 4 to 6 months would probably be fine. You can keep a record or a log noting the date you changed the strings, the brand and types of strings and also the gauge. Keep a little notepad or a piece of paper in your guitar case for this purpose and you'll never have to wonder when your strings need replacing. You can also take notes of any unusual set ups or problems that you encounter when using certain strings. This is a very helpful habit if you are still looking for the perfect set of strings to match your style of playing. Also, when buying guitar strings, consider buying in bulk. A 10 pack of strings will cost less per pack and you will always have a set of strings handy when you need it.

One sure way to check if you need new strings is to look for signs of wear. Twist one of your wound strings so that you can see the portion of the string that makes contact with the frets. If there is a flat spot or discoloration, then it's time to replace the strings.

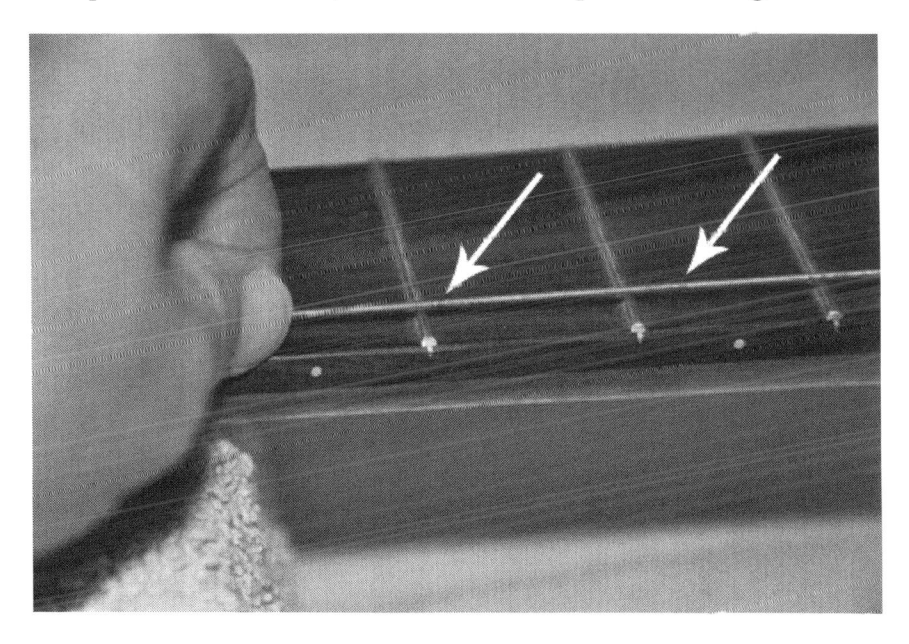

You can also run a clean piece of paper along the bottom of the string. If you see a bunch of dirt on the paper, that dirt is coming from the strings and it's probably time to replace them.

Not all guitar strings are created equal. Some strings are designed specifically for certain types of guitars. For instance, electric guitars require strings that are made out of white metals such nickel and nickel alloys. These metals react to the magnetics of the pick ups in an electric guitar. Classical guitar strings are made of nylon materials and would not sound good on a standard acoustic style or folk style guitar. And acoustic guitar strings come in a range of materials that will produce different sounds. Let's take a look a the most common types of guitar strings. These descriptions are not brand specific and most major guitar string manufacturers will have several different variations of the strings described below.

Phosphor Bronze
These strings are made of a steel core and are wrapped with a phosphor bronze alloy. They are very strong strings and will last longer than other sets. They will probably sound brighter or louder, not only because of the material they are made of, but because they pull harder on the bridge. This is something to be aware of. Keep an eye on the bridge of the guitar when you use these strings. If you have any signs of the bridge pulling away from the body of the guitar or the guitar top raising up from the stress, then consider going with a lighter gauge. Because the phosphor bronze strings pull so hard, it's wise to consider buying a lighter gauge right off the bat.

80/20 Bronze
These strings are made from 80% Copper and 20% zinc wire wrapped around the steel core wire. They will give you a nice bright sound, almost a little too bright for some people, but it all depends on what sound you want to produce. These strings are reasonably priced and they are more friendly on the bridge and neck than phosphor bronze strings because they tend to be a bit lighter.

Silk and Steel
Not many guitar players choose the silk and steel strings. These strings are made from a steel wire core, wrapped in silk which is wrapped in another material such as bronze or steel. Guitarists who play folk music and want a more mellow tone will often select this style of string. Some people don't like the sound and complain that they are too mellow and don't provide enough volume, but again, it depends on what type of music you like to play. Silk and steel strings are also great for beginners and kids because they are so

much more gentle on the fingers.

Coated Strings
Some strings will come with a polymer coating which protects the string form dirt and oils and makes them last a little bit longer. They are also a bit easier on the fingers as the wound strings don't seem as rough. They cost a little bit more, but they do last longer. Some guitarists don't like the sound as much, especially when you first put them on, because the polymer coating makes them sound a little bit more dull. They won't sound as mellow as the silk strings and some guitarists prefer a sound that is less bright.

Nylon Strings
Nylon strings are used for classical guitars. They won't sound very good if you put them on your acoustic. The bass strings, or the wound strings, are bronze or silver coated copper wound over a multi-filament nylon core. The treble strings are made of a durable nylon mono-filament and are generally clear. Some manufacturers will make black nylon treble strings and they are said to sound more pure and have more treble overtones than the clear strings. Nylon strings provide much less volume than steel strings but are very easy on the fingers. They are perfect for classical guitar style of playing. Also, nylon strings will not have a ball on the end and therefore will not work on an acoustic guitar that uses bridge pins. Instead the end is tied to the tie block located at the bridge.

Strings for the 12 String Guitar
These strings will come in all the varieties and types of materials found in the steel string line but will come with an extra set of strings, so to speak, to provide the octaves that you hear in a 12 string guitar.

Spend some time experimenting with different types of strings to find the sound and feel that you like best. Then stick with those strings. This is where taking notes comes in handy. Once you get some experience with different types of strings you can move on to more customized strings. For instance, there are strings with different materials used as a coating, or different metals used for the wound portion. Some of these custom strings are a bit more pricy, but it's fun to experiment to get the sound you like.

Installing Strings on a Classical Guitar

Classical guitars are a little bit different that other acoustic guitars and can be a little bit tricky. Because these guitars don't use pins on the bridge, the strings will not have a ball end. The strings will be tied to the bridge at a spot called the tie block.

With a new set of nylon guitar strings, at least for the base strings or the wound strings, one side of the string will be tightly wound and the other side will be wound a little bit loose. The tightly wound end will be installed at the bridge.

When you have all the strings removed, be careful that you don't lose the saddle piece as they are generally not glued on. The saddle will be slightly higher on one end. The higher end will align with the low bass strings, so make sure you place it in the proper direction.

To install a string, place the end of the string through the hole in the tie block and push it through until you have about 2 to 3 inches to work with. Bring the end of the string up and over the tie block, wrap it around the string once, then loop it over itself twice.

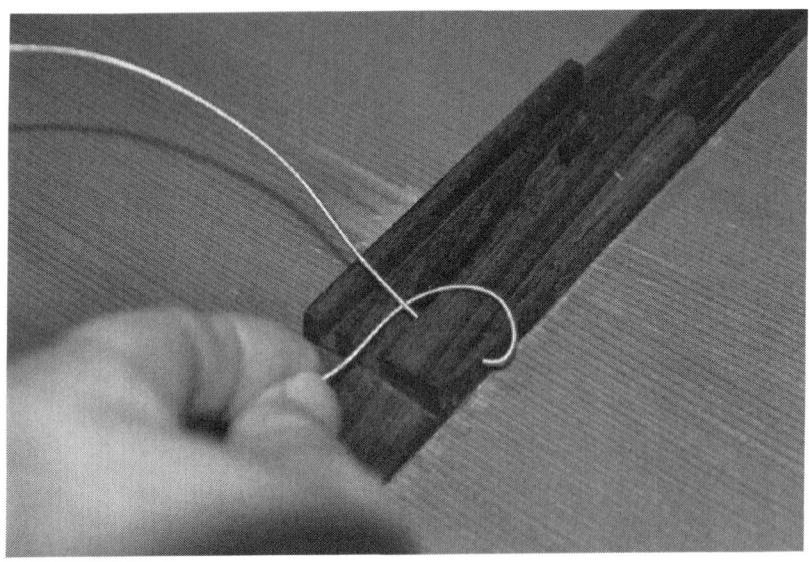

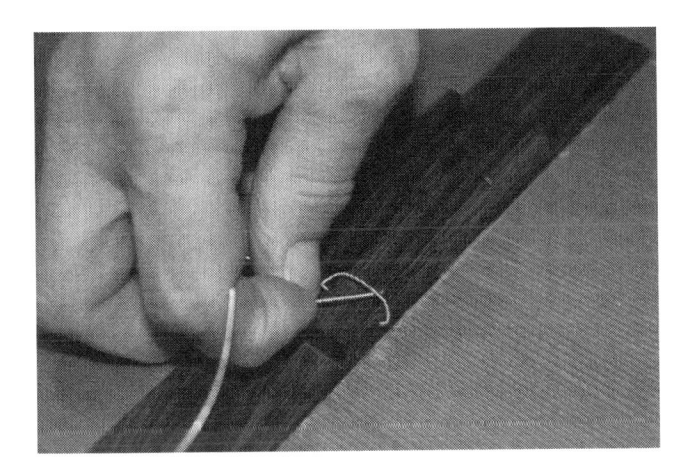

While holding down the twist that you have just created, pull the string tight. The twist must be set below edge of the tie block. If the entire knot is sitting on top of the tie block, the string could slip and break or pull off.

When installing the treble strings, or the bottom 3 strings, give them a couple of extra wraps before you pull them tight. This is because the strings are not wound and are made of nylon which can have a tendency to slip if they are not wound tight enough.

At the head stock, place the end of the string through the hole of the tuning post fro the front side towards the back.

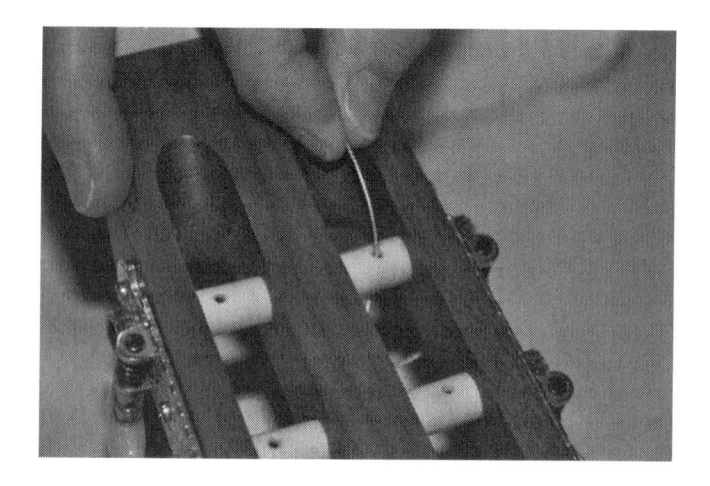

Bring the short end of the string up the back side of the post and loop it around the string going through the front of the tuning post so it forms a little "U" around itself. Next, take the short end and slip it through loop you just made on the back side of the post. Your basically tying a knot around the post.

Pull on both sides of the string until it tightens up and is secure on the post. Begin turning the tuning key to wind the string up and over the tuning post. Keep tension on the string with your free hand and bring the string up in pitch until is is close to standard. It doesn't have to be tuned as this point.

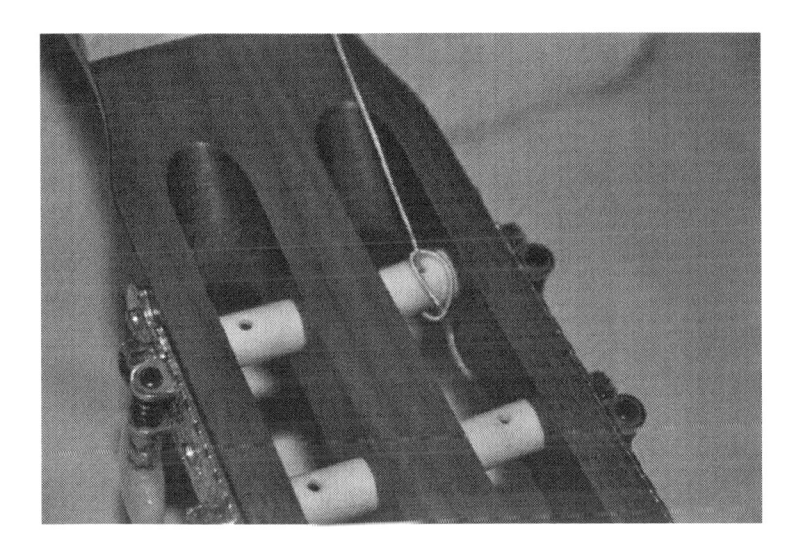

Continue installing the rest of the strings and allow them to stretch. Nylon strings will take a lot longer to stretch out because of the properties of the materials. You will notice that in order to bring it up to pitch it will take numerous twists of the tuning key, more than on a typical steel string guitar. To take some of the stretch out of the string, grab the strings with with your fingertips on one side and press against the string with your thumb from the other side.

Give it a good tug at several places along the length of the string. Bring the string back up to pitch and repeat the process. Do this several times or until the string seems to be holding its pitch.

Repeat this with all the other strings. Even when stretching the strings like this, you may notice that you will have to re-tune your guitar each day for several days and it takes the strings this long to stretch. Keep this in mind if you plan to play your guitar for an audience. Replace your strings several days before your performance or else you will be out of tune when it comes time to play.

Installing Strings on an Acoustic Guitar

Changing strings on a guitar that uses bridge pins is less complicated than the classical guitar strings, but still, a lot of people get a little confused about how the ball end should fit with the bridge posts. You may have encountered a pin being catapulted across the room as soon as you put tension on the string. There's a way to avoid that.

The pin is designed to hold the string in the bridge hole when there is tension place on the string. It does not hold the string in place until then. So, when you install the strings, do it in a way that keeps the strings loose. Here's how.

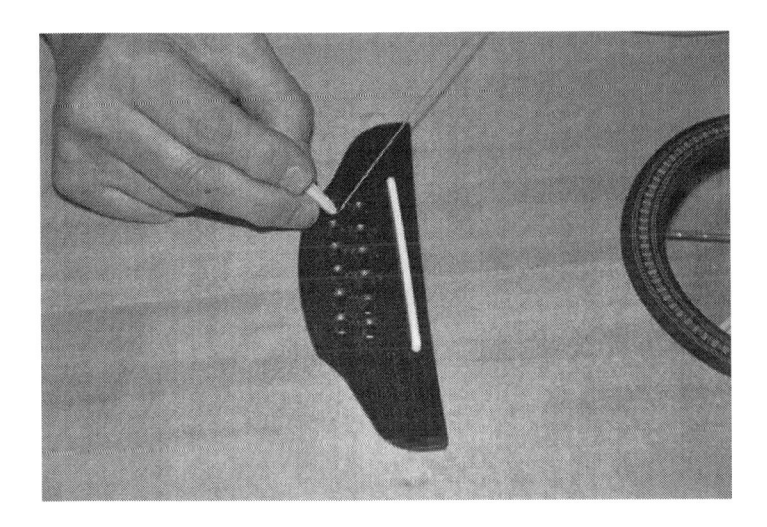

Place the ball end inside the bridge hold, then place the pin inside the hole. Make sure the hollowed out side of the pin is facing the string. When you put the pin in, the string should be slightly loose. While holding the pin down, give the string a slight tug. This will seat the ball end against the wood inside the guitar and the pin will hold it in place. At this point, it's actually easy to pull the pin back out and that's okay. Once you attache the string to the headstock and bring it up to pitch, the pressure will keep the pin secure and the pin will prevent the string from coming loose.

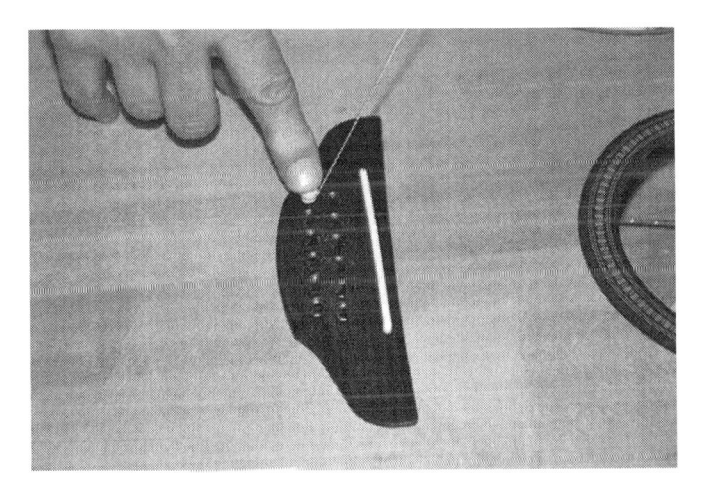

The next step is to wind the other end of the string around the tuning post. There are a number of ways to do this and guitarists all seem to have their special method for tying the string to make sure it is secure. Any of these methods will work but there are a few important things to remember.

At the headstock, the tuning post should turn counter clockwise for the top three strings and clockwise for the bottom three strings. In other words, they should wrap from the inside of the head to the outside.

Method 1:
Start with the hole in the tuning post angled at 45 degrees to the guitar. pull the string around the post once, hold it down with one finger behind the post, then take the end of the string and place it through the hole in the post. Pull it through all the way, then bend the end of the string to form a kink at the post. With this method, the first wind around the post is done. Simply continue winding the tuning post making sure the rest of the string winds down the tuning post, below the first wind.

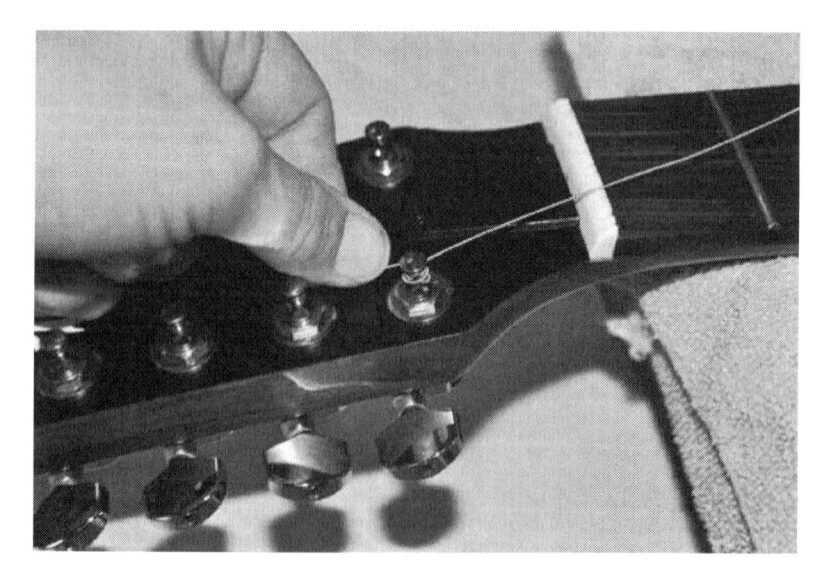

Method 2:

Measure the string at the point where it just passes the next tuning peg and bend it to place a kink in the string. Now pull the string back to get some slack and the string will stop at the tuning post right where you placed the bend.

Next, start winding the string making sure the tuning post is turning counter clockwise if it's a bass string and clockwise if it's a treble string. The first wrap should go over the end string and each wrap there after should go under the end string. This will cause the windings to pinch the string that extends out the tuning post, keeping it in place.

Installing Strings on a 12 String Guitar

Installing strings on a 12 string guitar is not much different than any other acoustic, but there are a few things you need to know to make sure the strings are installed correctly.

First thing you should realize is that the bridge on the 12 string is under a lot more pressure than a standard 6 string. This can cause the bridge to raise up from the guitar top, so it is something you should always be looking out for. Second, and also related to tension, you'll find that the thin G string is probably the first string to break if it is tuned too high, so be extra careful when tuning up this string. It would be nice if a set of strings came with an extra G string because, eventually it's going to break.

It's great if you can buy a set of strings that are color coded. This makes it much easier to match a pair as the thinner strings begin to look exactly alike. When you open the package of strings you will find the pairs wound together. Take out one pair at a time so you don't get them mixed up. The packaging will tell you which colors go where and if they are not color coded, then there may be a sticker on the string itself. Be sure to take that off before you install the string.

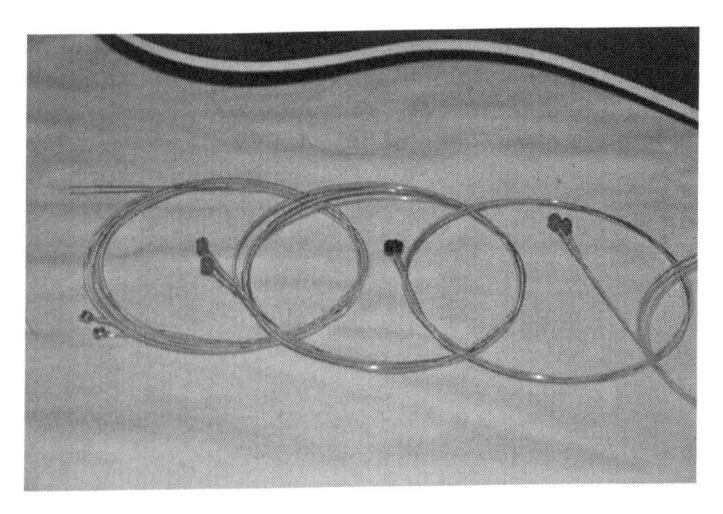

To install the strings, use the same methods discussed earlier in the section about stringing an acoustic guitar. The ball end of the string will fit in the bridge hole and the bridge pin will hold the string into place.

Start with the 6th string pair first, or the low E string. The thinner of the pair will be on the top, and the wound, thick E string will be install just below it.

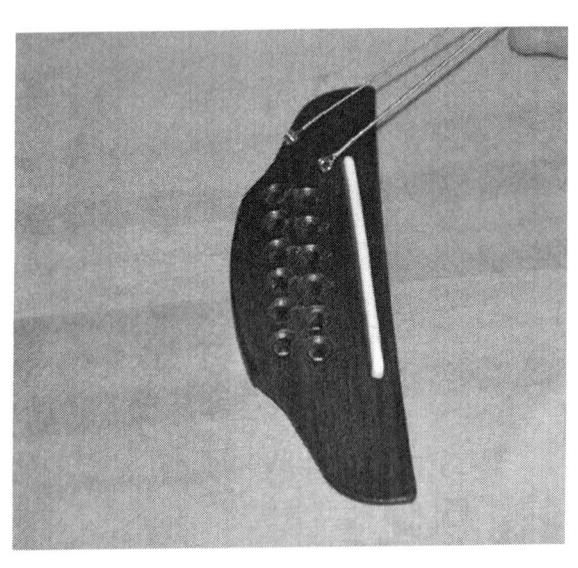

Wind the strings onto the tuning posts following the same instructions you learned earlier. Remember that the thinner strings will require morel windings around the post to keep it from slipping.

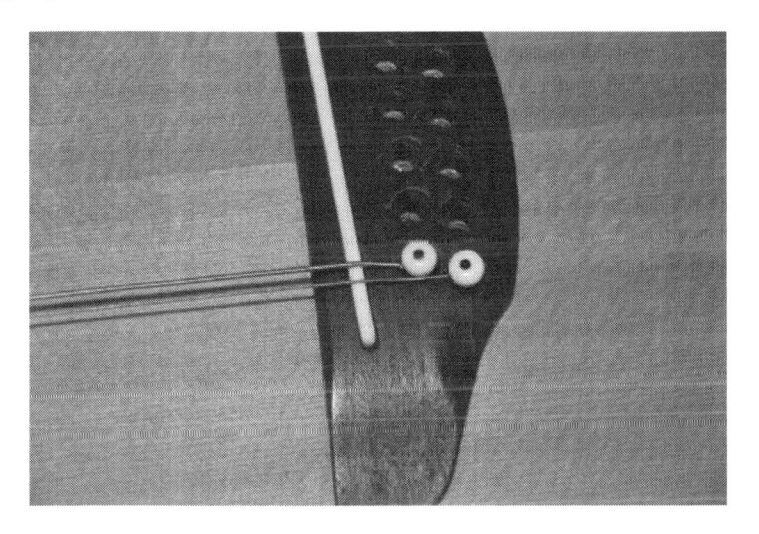

Next, move on to the 5th string pair. Just like the E strings, the thinner of the pair will be on top with the thicker string just below it. Install the strings on the bridge and on the tuning posts.

Continue this pattern with the 4th string and, for most string set, the 3rd string as well. When you are ready to install the 2nd and 1st string sets, it doesn't matter what order you go in, both strings are the same gauge.

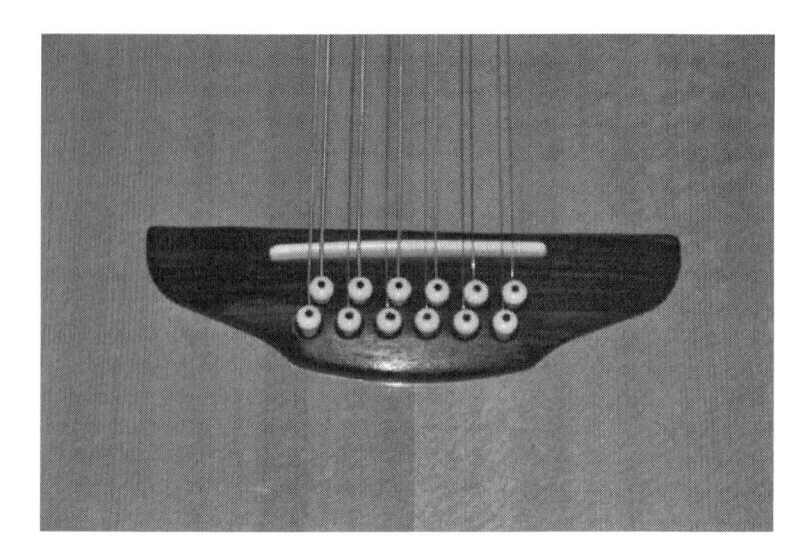

Be sure to stretch the strings gently while you are bringing them up to pitch. A great trick is to tune the thicker strings first, just as you would a 6 string guitar then, go back and tune the remaining strings. This trick will help prevent you from accidently tuning a string too high, especially that G string, and breaking one.

Read about how to tune your 12 string in the next section on how to tune a guitar.

After your new strings have been on the guitar a couple of days, check the tuning again as with all new strings, they will take a while to stretch completely

How to use a Digital Tuner

A digital tuner is by far the fastest, easiest and most accurate way to tune your guitar. Digital tuners come in a variety of styles. Most will use a microphone to hear the tone from your guitar. You simply set the tuner close enough so it is able to pick up the sound of your guitar. This is a good method but there is one problem with it. Sometimes, especially if you're in a noisy room, the tuner will pick up other sounds which can throw off the reading, causing you to do some guess work.

Most tuners will give you the option to connect directly to your guitar through the guitar's output. This will only work if you have a pickup on your acoustic guitar. This method cancels out the microphone so it won't pick up outside noises, giving you a much more accurate reading.

The third style of tuner uses the vibrations in the guitar. A piezo tuner clips to the headstock and picks up the vibrations or frequency and tells you if the tone is sharp or flat. This style of tuner is very inexpensive, easy to use (you just clip it on and clip it off) and gives a good, accurate reading. Just make sure the batteries are fresh.

Digital tuners will use either a needle, LED lights or an LCD display to indicate when you hit the correct pitch. The easiest to read are the kind with LED lights. If the light is red, the string is either flat or sharp, depending on where the red light it. If the light is green, your in tune. It's as easy as that. Needles tend to swing a little before they rest at an accurate reading and, although they are very accurate, it takes a little bit of practice to read them correctly.

Tuning Without a Tuner

This technique comes in handy hen you don't have your tuner or the batteries have run out. It's always best to tune to an electronic tuner especially when you are playing with other musicians. That way you all have the same reference point and your instruments will be tuned the same. But, if you're playing by yourself, you can tune the strings relative to each other and it will sound fine.

The first thing you need to do is to look at matching fretted notes with open notes, so if you start on the 6th string, or the low E string, Fretting that on the 5th fret produces an A note which is the same as the open 5th string. Next, fretting the 5th string on the 5th fret will produce a D note, the same as the open 4th string. Continuing on in the same pattern, fretting the 4th string on the 5th fret produces a G note which is the same as the open 3rd string. When we get to the 3rd string, to match the pitch of the 2nd string it must be fretted on the 4th fret. This matches the B note which is the same as the open 2nd string.

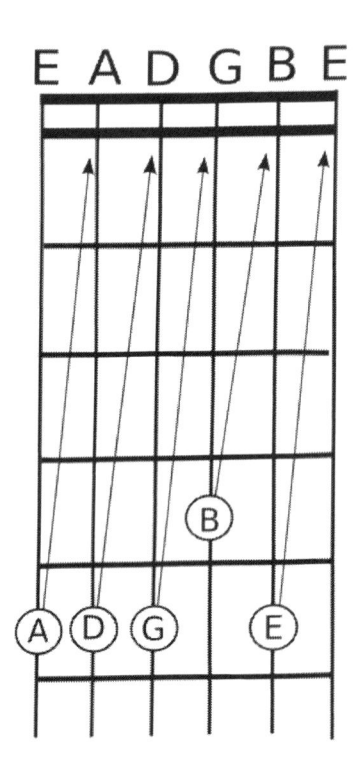

Now, for the 2nd string, go back to fretting it on the 5th fret. This will give you an E note, which is the same as the 1st string.

When you tune, it's always better to tighten the string instead of loosening it. When you tighten, you keep tension on the string whereas, when you're loosening it you can create slack which makes the string go out of tune later on when you're playing. Here's another benefit. Let's say the note is just a little bit sharp. Sometimes when a note is just slightly sharp, you can tell that it's out of tune, but you can't necessarily tell if it's sharp or flat. If you just loosen the string, lowering the tone so you know it's flat, then you can bring it back up to pitch. It's much quicker and easier to do this than to fiddle with tiny adjustments that don't seem to change the pitch.

Here's a great trick for training your ear to match the pitch of two strings on the guitar. Let's say the 1st string, the high E string, is out of tune. If you fret the 2nd string on the 5th fret to get your reference note, and play the two strings together, you will hear a wavy type of sound. Kind of like a wah-wah-wah-wah. These waves tell you that the two notes don't match and the bottom string is out of tune. A you turn the tuning key and bring the 1st string up in pitch to match the 2nd string, you will notice the wave will become shorter or sound slower. You want to try to get rid of it completely, so you hear no wave at all. That will show you that the two strings match and you are in tune. this is the most accurate way to match two pitches together without using a tuner.

To tune your guitar, you will combine the two things we just talked about. Start with the low E string, the 6th string, fret it on the 5th fret and match the pitch of the 5th string to that tone using the wave method. Continue doing this with each string until all your guitar strings are in tune.

There is one other trick you can use on the lower strings. Sometimes when you have lower notes, it's a little hard to hear the pitch to get the notes to match. So, one trick is to use harmonics. Harmonic tones are produced by lightly touching the string at the 5th or 7th fret and plucking the string to create a ringing tone, like a bell. Your finger must be directly on top of the fret rather than between the two frets. To create the harmonics for the first two strings, play the harmonic on the 6th string, 5th fret, then play the harmonic on the 5th string 7th fret. These two notes should match. If they don't, adjust the 5th string to match the 6th. Harmonics makes it easier to hear the wave. You can simply let the two strings ring, listen for the wave, and turn the tuning key until the wave disappears.

Tuning a 12 String

12 string guitars are a little more tricky but the same tuning methods apply. The easiest way, and the most accurate way to tune a 12 string is to use a digital tuner. This will take the guess work out of trying to figure out if the high string is the right note. I've broken a few strings in my time because I was tuning the thin string much too high.

Each group of two strings are tuned to the same note. For instance, the 11th and 12th strings are tuned to E, the 9th and 10th strings to an A, the 7th and 8th strings are tuned to a D; the 5th and 6th strings are tuned to G, the 3rd and 4th strings are tuned to a B, and lastly, the 1st and 2nd strings are tuned to E.

The bass strings, or the top 3 pairs, are tuned one octave apart. Meaning, the thinner string is one octave higher than the thicker string. The treble strings, or the bottom 3 pairs, are tuned to the exact same pitch.

But if you don't have a tuner handy, you can use the same method discussed above; using the low E string as a reference point, and tuning each string by fretting the previous string at the 5th fret. First, tune the very top string, the 12th string, one octave higher than the 11th string, the low E string. Next, fret the low E string at the 5th fret and use it as a reference point for the next pair of strings. Match the 9th string, or the low A, to the 11th string. Once you have that perfect, then tune its matching string, the 10th string one octave higher than the 11th. Continue in this fashion until all the strings are in tune.

Tips*: Tune the thick string first, then tune the thinner string to match the thick string. It is better to have the pairs tuned perfectly to each other to get a much cleaner sound.*

Because the strings are under so much tension on a 12 string, and if you don't want to worry about tuning your 12 string up too high, breaking the strings and causing a lot of stress on the bridge, tune the guitar down a whole step. So instead of tuning it to E, A, D, G, B, E you will tune it to D, G, C, F, A, D. This will take a lot of tension off the bridge. This is a great way to take care of your guitar especially if you don't play very often and it is perfect if you're playing alone. However, if you are going to play with other musicians, simply put a capo on the 2nd fret to bring it up to standard pitch.

Adjusting the Neck or Truss Rod

Adjusting the neck is one park of guitar maintenance that is commonly ignored or is not done because one, people don't understand what this adjustment is, or, two, they are afraid of doing permanent damage to their guitar. But, its also one of those things that's bound to effect nearly every guitar at some point simply because steel strings can exert up to 200 pounds of pressure on the neck. To make the situation worse, is the fact that the neck can be thrown out of alignment in a number of ways such as wear on the saddle and nut, or humidity changes. Each one of those changes can have its own symptoms that many guitar players are not aware of.

For instance, you could be playing your guitar and you notice a lot of buzzing between the first and the 5th frets. Or, you might have a guitar which gives you buzzing notes when you play between the 12th fret and the 17th fret. Both of these are symptoms of a neck that needs adjusting. There are actually a lot of other scenarios too, such as bad intonation or high action. Many of these problems can be traced back to a neck that is out of adjustment, so before moving on to adjusting action and intonation, you want to make sure the truss rod and neck are adjusted properly.

What should you look for when determining if your guitar's neck needs adjusting? First, let's talk about what a properly adjusted neck should look like. Some people may think that the neck of the guitar should be completely flat, but this is a common mistake. It is true that when a guitar is manufactured the neck is flat and all the frets are perfectly level and in alignment with one another. However, once you put the strings on and begin exerting that 200 pounds of pressure on the neck, it will naturally bow forward just a little bit.

A well adjusted guitar will have a very slight forward bow. If your guitar is completely flat, you will probably notice a buzzing when you play near the nut or up on the higher frets. If the neck has too much of a forward bow, the action will be too high. It will be difficult to play and will probably sound slightly out of tune when you play a chord due to the fact that you have to depress the strings so far down. Another common problem is a back bow in the neck. This problem should be easy to see because no matter where on the fret board you play the guitar, you will experience buzzing in the strings because the strings will be riding too close to the frets.

An accurate way to check the bow of the guitar neck is to use a 12" or 18" steel ruler. Place the ruler on top of the frets. Place it so that it butts up against the nut. On a properly adjusted guitar, the ruler should contact the first few frets and the last few frets at both ends of the ruler and there should be a very slight gap between the ruler and the frets in between.

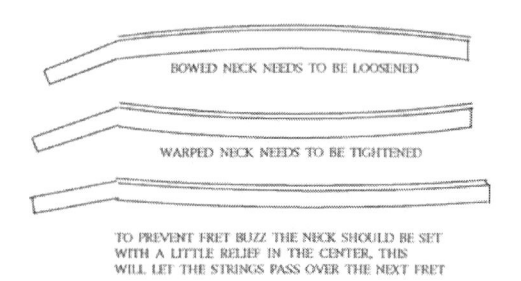

BOWED NECK NEEDS TO BE LOOSENED

WARPED NECK NEEDS TO BE TIGHTENED

TO PREVENT FRET BUZZ THE NECK SHOULD BE SET WITH A LITTLE RELIEF IN THE CENTER. THIS WILL LET THE STRINGS PASS OVER THE NEXT FRET

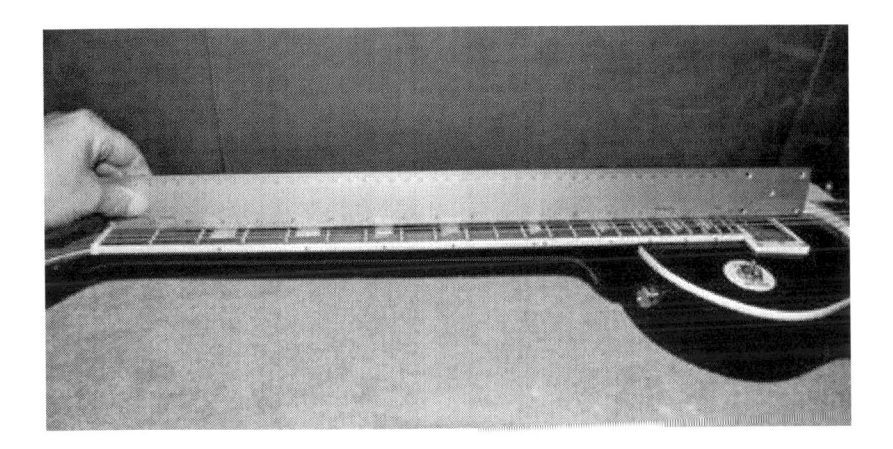

If you place the ruler on the frets and you find that the ruler actually rocks back and forth a little bit, then your guitar neck has a back bow to it. Meaning, the ruler will be touching the frets in the middle of the neck but not touching the frets on either end.

Another way of check the bow in the neck is to do a sight check. Hold the guitar in front of you and look straight down the guitar neck from the head stock. What you should see are nice straight strings and a near perfectly straight surface of the neck. If there are any irregularities in the bow of the neck, you're going to be able to see it when you inspect the neck this way. The problem with this method is that your eyes can be quickly deceived by any irregularities in the frets themselves so you shouldn't rely on this method completely. It is a good system if you are in a store or purchasing a used guitar and you don't have an 18 inch ruler handy, but remember, it's only a rough estimate.

How much of a bow should the guitar neck have?

There is an easy and practical way to check to see if the truss rod actually needs adjustment.

Place a capo on the first fret.

Next, press down on the 6th string at the 12th fret.

While pressing on the 12th fret, with your other hand press down on the string at the 5th fret. If you can hear the string tap against the frets then you know there is some space between the fret and the string and this tells you that your guitar's neck has a forward bow to it. If you hear no tapping noise and the string touches the frets, then the neck is too straight or may have a slight backward bow. In this case, the truss rod needs a slight adjustment.

How do you know if you have too much space, or too much forward bow? One easy way to measure is by using a business card and a credit card. With the capo on the first fret and your finger on the 12th fret, a business card should fit in the gap nicely. If it does, then the neck has just enough forward bow. A credit card should not quite fit into the space without hitting or lifting the strings a little. If you can get a credit card or more in that space, then your guitar has a little too much forward bow and the truss rod needs a slight adjustment.

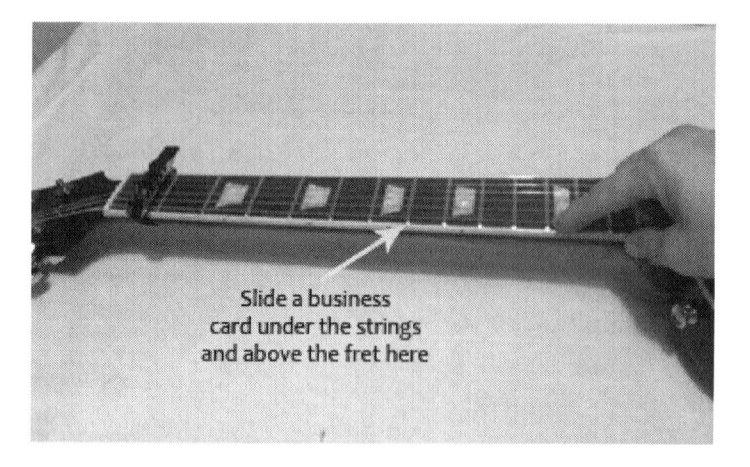

Slide a business card under the strings and above the fret here

If you determine that the truss rod needs an adjustment it is more than likely that it only needs a very small adjustment. Follow the steps below carefully and you'll be able to adjust your guitar's neck without breaking it.

WARNING: *Be careful when doing this adjustment. The truss rod*

is what keeps your guitar in one piece under the intense pressure of the strings. If your truss rod breaks, your guitar breaks. Adjust at your own risk.

On acoustic guitars you can find the truss rod nut at the head of the guitar located under a little cover or inside the soundhole.

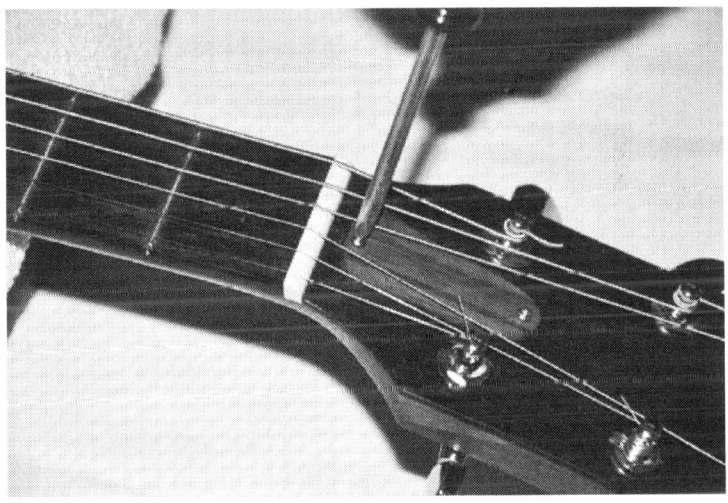

The adjustment will be made with a hex key, also known as an allen wrench or with a special truss rod tool that will come with most new guitars. Place the wrench in the truss rod bolt and turn it in the desired direction 1/4 turn at a time.

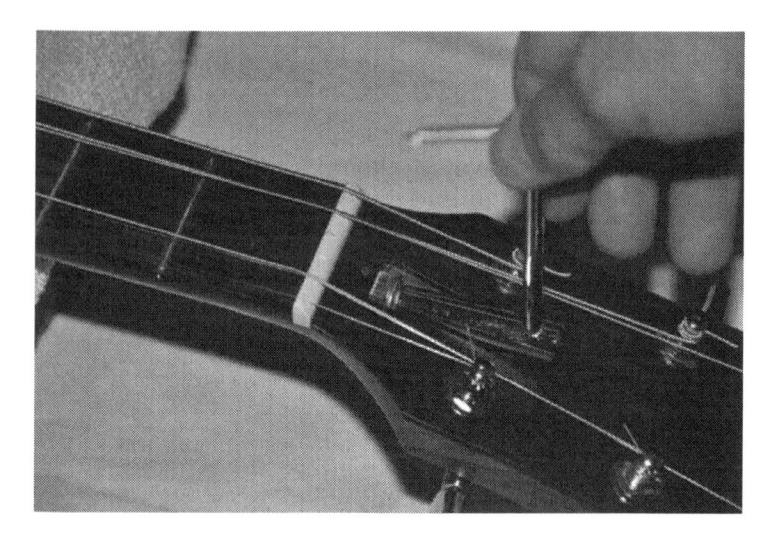

A quarter turn will have a dramatic effect on the guitar neck. Whatever you do, don't go turning it a full turn in either direction. If you find it difficult to turn the nut, and you feel like you have to force it to get it to turn, STOP! Don't do it. The truss rod could be broken or seized up inside the neck. This is when you should take your guitar to a professional technician.

If your guitar has too much forward bow, and your strings are too high off the fret board, then loosen the truss rod by turning the nut 1/4 turn counter-clockwise, or to the left. If your strings are too close to the frets or the neck has a backward bow, then tighten the truss rod by turning it 1/4 turn clockwise, or to the right.

After adjusting the truss rod, allow the guitar to sit for 10 to 15 minutes. Then tune the guitar and check the height of the strings again using the method shown earlier. If your guitar is in good shape, then one or two adjustments should be all it needs.

This adjustment will greatly improve the action of your guitar, but it is only the first adjustment in a complete setup.

Adjusting the Action

Action refers to the height of the strings above the frets. You don't want the action to be too high or too low and you want to adjust it to fit your playing style. If the action is too low, the strings will hit the frets when they are played causing a buzzing sound. If the action is too high, it will be difficult to press the strings down, especially on the higher frets. You will sometimes have to press the string down so far that it changes it's pitch causing the guitar to sound out of tune.

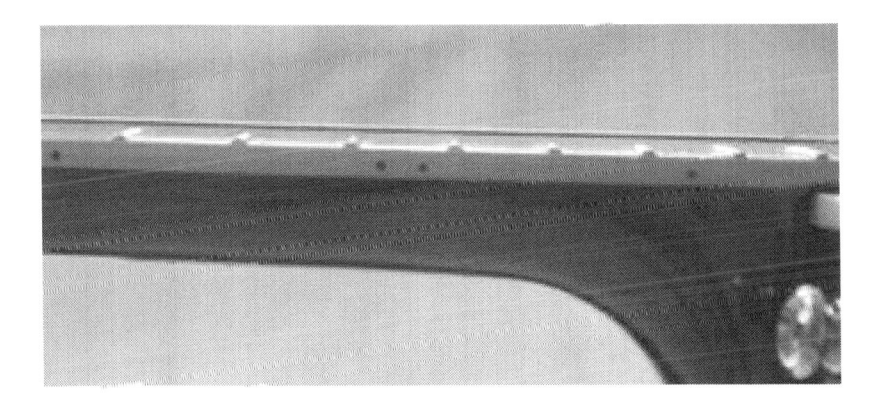

Different guitars playing styles require different action settings, for instance, if you play heavy rhythm guitar such as bluegrass or folk, then you may prefer an action that is slightly high. This will allow the strings a larger vibration pattern giving them more volume without hitting the frets. If you like to play finger picking, or blues, or any music that requires speed, especially at the higher frets, then you will like a low action. You will want to get your action as low as possible without buzzing on the frets.

There are several factors that will effect the action and we have already covered a couple of adjustments that will help with any action problems. The first one was re-gluing the bridge. If the bridge is raising off the top of the guitar, it will cause the action to be way too high. So, ensuring that your bridge is properly in place will allow you to get the action adjustment you want.

The next factor is the truss rod. If your truss rod is adjusted to the proper relief, then the action should be just about right.

Next factor is the saddle height. This is one of the easier adjustments that you can make if your action is too high. Sanding away a millimeter from the bottom of the saddle may be just enough to get the action at the perfect spot. But you have to be careful to sand it off correctly; take off too much and you may have to replace the saddle.

Adjusting the Saddle Height

You don't have to remove the strings in order to remove the saddle. You can loosen all the strings just enough to get the saddle out of the bridge. The saddle of acoustic guitars are not glued on and you should be able to pull it out using only your fingers. If it's too tight in the groove, you can use pliers to gently pull it up.

If your guitar is an acoustic/electric, you will most likely see the pickup laying under the saddle. Be careful with these as they are delicate. You can lift it up, but there will be a wire attached to it. Handle it gently so you don't bend it or break the wires.

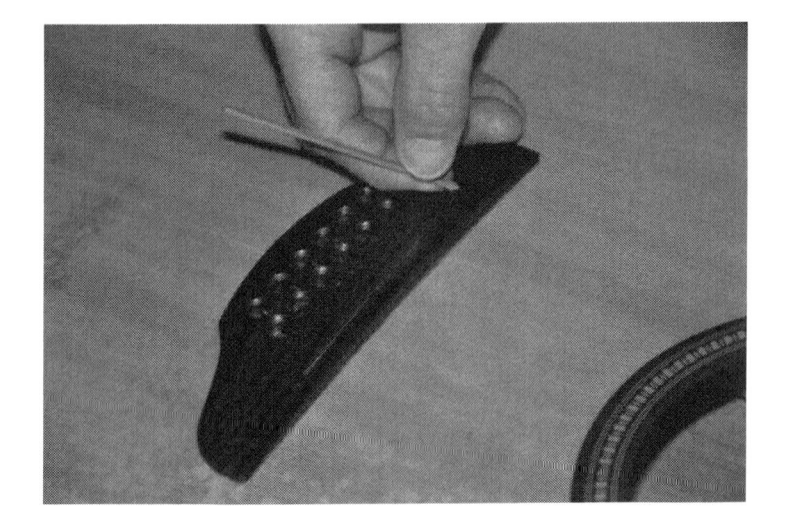

You will need a very fine piece of sandpaper and a very smooth surface. Glueing some sandpaper on a piece of plexiglass or on a smooth ceramic tile works very well.

While holding the saddle at a very even angle, move it back and forth gently on the sandpaper. Be careful not to tilt the saddle in one direction or another as this will cause the bottom to become uneven. Also, be sure to apply even pressure on both ends while you sand it. A good way to ensure even pressure is to flip the saddle around every couple of strokes.

Be sure to always, sand a little, then check the adjustment. To check it quickly, place the saddle back into the bridge then bring the 3rd and 4th strings up to pitch to place tension on the neck. Check the saddle height again to see if it is the way you like it. If not, loosen the strings, remove the saddle and sand off a tiny bit more, then re-check the adjustment. Do this until you are satisfied with the saddle height and you don't here any buzzing from the strings.

What if you sand off too much or the saddle is too low? You can either purchase a new saddle and start from scratch, or you can add a thin layer of material under the saddle to raise it slightly. The best material to use is very thin polyurethane, however, not everyone has this laying around. Luthiers will use pick guard material which they have handy, but what about the do-it-yourself luthiers? A very thin piece of paper, such as tracing paper, is a good place to start.

Using the saddle as a template, cut a piece of paper to fit perfectly inside the saddle groove. This may take a couple of tries, but you want it to fit perfectly into the bottom of the groove without any going up the sides. Try one layer at first and check the saddle height. If it's still too low, add one more layer of paper.

If you have an acoustic/electric, the paper must go UNDER the pickup to it doesn't interfere with the signals received from the vibration of the bridge.

This is somewhat of a tedious process, but it is well worth it. This part of the setup will last a long time and you will love how your guitar plays once you get it just right. Remember, if you mess this up, it's not the end of the world, especially if you guitar is a common brand. You can take your old saddle to the music store and if they don't have one in stock, most guitar shops will be happy to order one for you.

Adjusting the Nut Height

Another component of the guitar that can effect the action is the nut height. If the nut is too high, the action at the top few frets will be too high. When this is the case, the strings are difficult to push down at the first fret, and will have to stretch to the point where they sound out of tune. If the nut is too low, you may experience buzzing at the first fret, especially when strumming loud.

The nut can be adjusted in the same manner as the saddle, in fact this is the easiest way to adjust a nut that is too high across all the strings. However, if one string is a little too high, and the other strings are fine, then the individual slot hight must be adjusted. First let's cover how to remove the nut and adjust it's height, then re glue it into place.

Removing the Nut

Removing the nut is not as easy as removing the saddle as the nut is glued into place. Follow these instruction carefully to remove the nut without damaging the nut or the guitar and its finish.

You will need:

A razor blade or craft knife (x-acto knife)

A small hammer

A small block of wood

A small chisel

It's easiest to do this without having the strings in the way. Loosen the strings enough to pull them to the sides so the nut is completely exposed. It's best to leave the strings on the guitar as you will need to put them back into place to check the nut height.

Often, around the edges of the nut will be varnish. In order to prevent this varnish from cracking and pealing away from the surface of the guitar, trim around all the edges of the nut with a razor blade. You are basically cutting through the varnish coating.

Next, you need to knock the nut out of it's slot. Place a small block of wood at the first fret, against the side of the nut. Tape the block with a hammer gently and repeatedly until you feel the nut come loose. You can place the block of wood on the other side of the nut and tap from there too. It may take a little bit of work to get it off, but be patient, you don't want to crack the nut. Before you start sanding down the nut, you will want to clean out the groove. Using a small chisel or a small, flat file or razor blade, remove any excess glue from the groove. Be careful not to remove any of the wood from the bottom or sides of the groove.

Once you have the nut removed and the nut slot cleaned, use the same methods described in the section on saddle height to sand away a very small amount from the bottom of the nut. Remember to sand a little, then test your adjustment by placing the nut in its groove, then check the height of the strings again. Do this procedure until the strings are at just the right height on the first fret. Bring the strings up to pitch and test for any string buzz.

Once you have it adjusted the way you like it, you need to glue it back into place. Apply a small amount of super glue to the bottom of the nut slot then put the nut back into place. It doesn't require much glue because the pressure from the strings will help hold it into place. Now, tune your guitar back up to pitch and you should be good to do.

Adjusting the Nut Slots
Adjusting each individual nut slot is a little more difficult and it may be something you want to let a guitar technician do. To do it

properly, you will need a set of nut files. If you want to invest in a set, they are not too expensive; anywhere from $12 to $25 for a set. It's best to use a set designed for this purpose because each slot has its own special file. The file will be the perfect width to accommodate the thickness of the string. For instance the file for the 6th string notch will be fairly thick, while the file for the 1st string will be extremely thin. The file will also create a rounded groove so the string can rest perfectly without snagging on the edges.

Some do-it-yourselfers have used a small jewelers file or a rat-tail file to do this job. This method will work, but will not give you the precision that the specialty files will. If you end up making the notch too wide, the string will have a tendency to slide back and forth in the slot and this may cause clicking noises when you play, especially when you bend the strings. You'll notice it more when you tune your guitar. If you hear a clicking noise when bringing a string up to pitch, it may be snagging on the edges of the nut.

As you can see, it's best to use the proper tools for this particular job. If you don't want to invest in the tools, you can take the guitar to a certified technician and they will be sure to do the job right. But if you do want to try it yourself, purchase the files and give it your best shot. If you completely destroy the nut, you can always take it into a technician for a nut replacement. This type of job will generally cost you around $100 and may include a complete set up. So, if you don't get it right, it's not the end of the world or the end of your guitar. Just the end of your $100.

Adjusting the Intonation

The last thing you should check when doing a complete setup of your acoustic guitar is to check the intonation.

If you've ever played a guitar that was perfectly tuned, but sounded out of tune when you play different chords, or when played on higher frets, then you've played a guitar with bad intonation. A guitar should play true to its note on every string and every fret of the neck. If it doesn't, then it has intonation problems. On a guitar with proper intonation, the distance between the nut and the 12th fret will be exactly the same as the distance between the 12th fret and the saddle leaving compensation for the thickness of the strings. And when I use the word "exactly" I mean "exactly". A well manufactured guitar will have no intonation problems, so this is actualy an adjustment that you may never have to make, but it's a good idea to understand what it is so you recognize the problem if it should occur.

Intonation adjustments are traditionally done at the saddle by adjusting the length of the string. On most electric guitars this adjustment is a simple turn of a screw, but an acoustic guitar is not equipped with the mechanics to do such a simple adjustment, so it has to be done with a little more care and finesse.

Usually nylon string guitars don't have as much of a problem with intonation due to the material used on construct the strings and how that material affects the vibration of the string. But, this method will work on any style acoustic guitar.

The best way to check the intonation on your guitar is to test it with an accurate digital tuner. You will be comparing the pitch of an open string with the pitch of the same string played at the 12th fret. They should be exactly one octave apart. If the note at the 12th fret is sharp, or higher, the the string is too short and needs to be lengthened. If the the note at the 12th fret is flat, or too low, the string is too long and needs to be shortened. So, how do you lengthen or shorten the vibration distance of the string if there is nothing to move?

This adjustment is done by changing the crown of the saddle. The crown is the spot on the top of the saddle where the string contacts the saddle and stops vibrating. Adjusting the saddle is a tricky job and should be done with a patient hand. Again this may be one of those jobs you might want to leave to a technician, but if you want to give it a try, here are the steps.

You will be filing away very small portions of the saddle and if you over do it, you will end up having to buy yourself a new saddle, which again is not a big deal. So, again, use the basic rule of thumb: small adjustments then check your measurements. To adjust the saddle, use a very small, fine file or an emery board. Lift the appropriate string away from the saddle enough to allow working room for the string that need adjustment.

If the intonation is sharp and string needs to be lengthened, then file away a very small amount of material at the front of the saddle. This will cause the vibration stopping point to move back very slightly resulting in a longer string or longer vibration distance. Work in very small increments, just a stroke or two, then check the intonation again. You may find that after making an adjustment you will have to bring the string back up to standard tuning and then check the pitch on the 12th fret again. Do this until the intonation is perfect. Repeat this procedure for each string until your guitar is just right.

If the string is too long, meaning, the pitch at the 12th fret is too low, or flat, then you have a more difficult problem to fix. The only way you could really fix this yourself is to purchase a new saddle and start from scratch. See the section in this book about replacing the saddle If this doesn't work, you will have to take your guitar into a luthier. A good guitar technician will be able to assess the situation and see if the saddle slot needs to be re-routed or if the bridge needs to be replaced to compensate for the intonation problem. Generally, on a decent guitar (one that hasn't been beat up too much) the intonation won't be off by much and if it is slightly flat, and you may find the guitar acceptable as it isd. In fact, the human ear will recognize a tone that is sharp much easier than recognizing a tone that is flat. So playing a guitar with flat intonation may not be noticeable to your audience. Also, an acoustic guitar by nature will never be perfect. There are too many variables that change the tone of the guitar such as climate. Strive to set up the intonation to near perfection and you will have a very nice sounding guitar.

A note about intonation on an acoustic guitar. It doesn't have to be perfect! There is something to be said about the character of the acoustic guitar and its slight imperfections. If you check the intonation and it sounds "close enough" then it is best to leave it. Going through the hassle making tiny adjustments to the saddle at the risk of ruining the saddle to get the intonation to absolute perfection is just kind of silly. This adjustment should be saved for the guitars where the intonation is noticeably off and adversely affects the way the guitar sounds when it is played. As mentioned earlier, if you own a decent guitar, the intonation will most likely be fine.

Final Check

Now that you have finished all the necessary steps of a set up, you should to a final check and cleaning.

Bring all the strings up to standard pitch. Play each string at every fret one at a time. You want to check for buzzing or any other sounds that are "off". Hopefully, your guitar will sound just fine after replacing the strings and taking good care of it.

Play some of your favorite songs for a while and play a variety of music. So some heavy strumming with some bar chords and listen for any unusual noises. Play some basic finger picking patterns and pay attention to the east of pressing down the strings at the first few frets. Then play some scales at the higher frets and listen for buzzing or intonation problems. Also, pay attention to how the action feels when you're playing scales at the higher frets. You want it to feel easy and comfortable, almost effortless.

If you've done the set-up procedure properly, your guitar will be playing just the way to like it.

Purchasing a Guitar

Buying a Second Hand Guitar

There are some very good reasons for buying a used guitar one of them being price. A gently used guitar that is less than 5 years old will usually sell for half of what it costs new. Also, older guitars, especially those more than 10 years old have had the chance to age and mellow allowing sounds to emerge that you don't hear on a new guitar. Older guitar are sometimes made from woods that are no longer available, such as brazilian rosewood.

It's easy to find a variety of used guitars on the market. The guitar seems to be the first thing people let go when they are cleaning out their closet or are in need of quick cash. You can benefit from this and get a great deal on an acoustic guitar if you know what to look for.

If you are new to buying a guitar, don't make the mistake of buying on impulse or buying the first decent guitar you see. Spend time, a lot of time, in your local music store playing a variety of guitars. Play the expensive guitars to get a good idea of what a well made guitar should sound and feel like. Play the cheap guitars so you can have a good comparison between the two. Jot down the names and model numbers of the guitars you like, then do some research to find out how much those guitars are going for used. In addition to playing the new guitars, ask if there are used guitars for sale at the shop and play a few of them to learn the differences between a new, just from the factory sound, and an older, broken in sound. Basically, do your research before you buy.

Cracks
Carefully inspect the entire surface of the guitar and look for any cracks in the wood. You also want to check for cracks at the seams. Is the top of the guitar separating from the sides? Is the neck separating from the body? Look for the tell tale signs of the finish cracking at the seams. Cracks in the finish are the first sign but it may not mean the guitar is doomed. If a guitar is dry, small cracks may begin to appear. This can be remedied by bringing the guitar back up to its proper humidity level. We will discuss humidity later in this book. If you see a crack in the seam large enough to slide a pick into, then it may not be something you want to purchase unless your willing to take it to a professional for repairs.

The Bridge
Check the edge of the bridge where it meets the guitar surface. If there is a gap, this is a sign that the bridge is pulling away from the guitar and may need to be replaced or removed and re-glued. This entire procedure is covered in this book.

The Headstock
Make sure the tuning keys are working properly and turn easily. Check for any cracks in the wood at the headstock and look for cracks at the top of the neck. Check the nut to make sure that it is not broken or cracked. If it is, it will have to be replaced.

The Fretboard

Check for wear on the frets under the strings. Worn out frets, indentations where the strings make contact, may cause tuning or intonation problems and a guitar with this condition will eventually need a re-fretting job. This is not necessarily a deal breaker, but is something to consider. Also, run your fingers along the sides of the neck. If you can feel the edges of the frets protruding past the edges of the neck, the guitar was probably not stored properly and has become dry. Usually bringing the humidity up will fix this, but it could also mean a re-fretting job.

The Neck

Look down the neck from the top of the guitar and check for even frets and a straight fretboard. Then look down the side edge of the neck to see how much bow is in the neck. If you hold down the 6th string at the 1st fret with one hand, and at the 12th fret with the other, you should see a slight gap between the fret and the string at the 6th fret. If there is too much of a gap, then it may only need a truss rod adjustment which will be covered in this book. But if the neck seems warped, or twisted, then that is a more serious problem. Also check to make sure the fretboard is not raised up at the frets closest to the sound hole. This problem is more difficult to fix yourself and it may need a neck reset which is a $200 to $300 job.

After reading this book and learning to do minor repairs and general maintenance, you will be able to assess whether or not you want to buy a guitar that needs a little work. You will have a basic understanding of what to look for, how it can be fixed and whether or not you can fix it yourself.

Buying a New Guitar

When you buy a new guitar you can be sure that there will be no damage such as dings or cracks. If you buy from a reputable guitar shop the guitar will most likely be set up, tuned and ready to play. Many guitar shops will allow you to bring in the guitar within 60 to 90 days for another setup free of charge. This is a great deal because it allows you to determine what your playing style is and you can let the guitar technician know if you want the action set higher or lower.

When looking for a new guitar take plenty of time to select the guitar that is right for you. Determine what your budget will be before you shop. If you set your budget to under $1000 that doesn't mean you shouldn't play the more expensive guitars. You should play a variety of guitars to get a good understanding of what makes a guitar expensive and what an affordable guitar features. Also play the less expensive guitars. You may be surprised to find that the guitar you like best is less expensive than you might have expected.

Don't purchase a guitar based on looks. Many guitar makers will add ornamentation such as inlays on the neck and headstock, which add to the price of the guitar but not necessarily the quality. And, just because a guitar is beautiful, or unique looking, doesn't mean that you will enjoy playing it, or that is perfect for you. Besides, guitars are not decorations. They should actually be stored in a case rather than constantly on display.

To sum it up, take your time, days or weeks or longer, selecting your new guitar, stay within your budget and be prepared to take good care of your new instrument for the first few years while the wood of the guitar goes through its curing process. The information in this book will teach you how to take care of your guitar during this vulnerable period.

Setting Up a Brand New Guitar

Most of the time, if you purchase a new guitar from a good dealer or music shop, you won't have to deal with setting up a new guitar. They will do it for you. New guitars that come right out of the box need to be set up and if you purchase a guitar from a shop that doesn't do it for you, then you will need to do it yourself. A set-up on a brand new guitar is almost identical to a set-up on any other guitar, but the nice thing is that you can be assured nothing is broken, all parts are new and the job will go much smoother and easier. Much of the information in this section has already been covered, but if you just purchased a new guitar, go through it and follow the procedures.

Check the bridge height. The bridge saddle on a new guitar will often come with shims under it causing the saddle to be very high. This, of course causes the strings to sit high over the fretboard, or high action. Fixing the bridge is a simple procedure on a new guitar. your first step is to remove the strings from the bridge. You don't need to take the strings all the way off and there is an easy way to do this. Loosen all the strings so there is a good amount of slack. Next, place a capo on the first fret. This will keep the strings in place on the tuning keys while you remove them from the bridge. This saves a lot of time when putting the strings back on.

Next, remove the pins from the bridge. Keep track of them as they tend to roll off the table and disappear forever. It's a good habit to place screws and other small parts in a plastic bag while you're working on the guitar so you know where they are at all time. Once you the pins out you should be able to pull the strings out easily. Move the strings off to the side carefully making sure you don't tangle them all up.

The bridge saddle should simply lift out of place. It is not generally held together with glue. Check inside the bridge to see if there are any shims or small strips of material. If there are, remove them. This may be all you have to do to get the saddle to the proper position.

CAUTION: *If your guitar is an electric acoustic be very careful. The pick-up for the electronics is often located under the saddle. When lifting anything out of the slot under the saddle, use extreme caution to avoid any damage to the pick-up.*

After removing shims, if you find them, place the saddle back into the guitar, replace the strings and tune it up. Check it again to see if the action is better. . A good way to measure the proper height is to take a quarter or similar coin and, with the strings installed, place the quarter on top of the frets at about the 9th fret. If your strings are not touching the coin, they are too high. You can lower the bridge farther by sanding it down at the bottom. See the chapter on bridge repair to read exactly how to do this. At this point in the adjustment process, the height of the strings can remain a little high because there are other adjustments that still need to be made that will effect the string height. So, with the coin in place, the strings should be just barely above the coin.

The next adjustment that will need to be made is tension on the neck or truss rod adjustment. When guitars are shipped, there is no tension on the truss rod and this will create a slight forward bow in the neck. Even though you want to have a tiny bow in the neck, usually, a truss rod with no tension will create a little too much bow, causing the strings to be too high off the fret. The truss rod nut will be located at either end of the neck and can be adjusted with a hex key wrench. Turn the truss rod clockwise 1/4 turn to tighten it, then check the action of the strings again using your coin. Even a slight adjustment of 1/4 turn will make a significance difference in the neck bow.

After you adjust the bridge saddle and truss rod, play each string at each fret individually and check for buzzing. If this is a brand new guitar and you made your adjustments very carefully, you shouldn't get any buzzing. If you do, see the section in this book about how to fix buzzing strings.

Other Hardware Adjustments

Although acoustic guitars are primarily made of wood and glue, there are still pieces that are held on with bolts and screws. These bolts and screws will work themselves loose over time and need attention when you're doing maintenance on your guitar. Tightening a bolt or screw is simple but there are a few things to keep in mind when doing so. Plus, if you have an acoustic/electric guitar there are some things you can do to keep the electronics in good working order.

At the headstock the nuts and screws holding the tuning posts and tuning keys will often come loose. Each time you do maintenance on your guitar, tighten these nuts using the proper size wrench or socket. Turn the nut until it is just firm enough to not come loose or rattle. Do not over-tighten as this may cause the wood to compress and, in worse cases, crack.

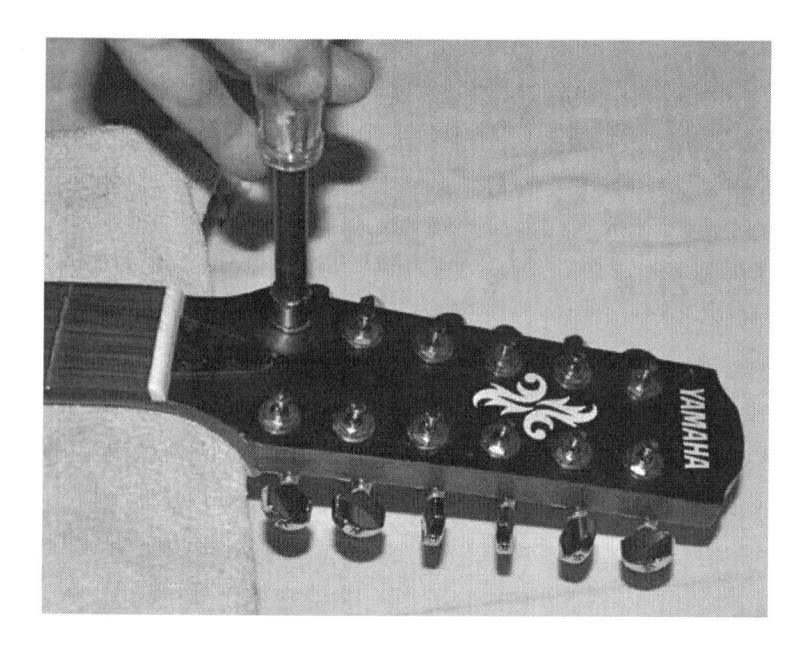

Check the strap holders to make sure the screw is tight and they are secure. This is as simple as tightening the screw with the proper size screwdriver and it will prevent damage to the body of the guitar caused by a loose strap pin.

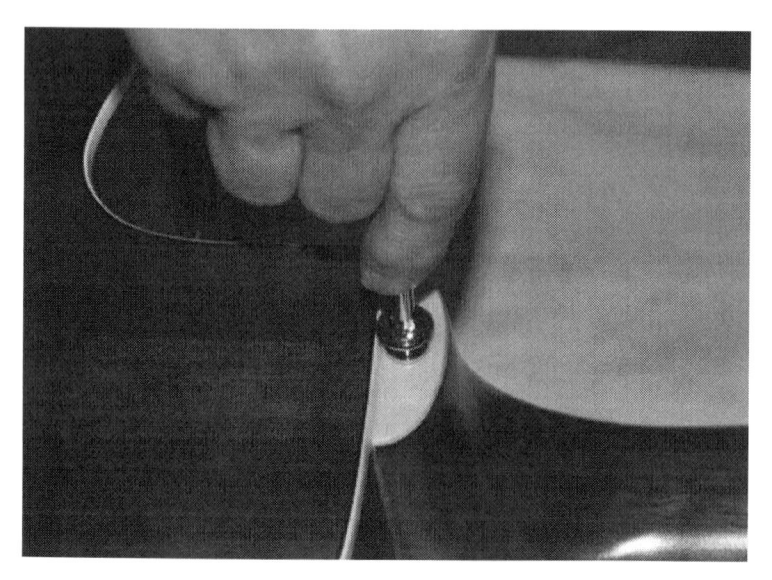

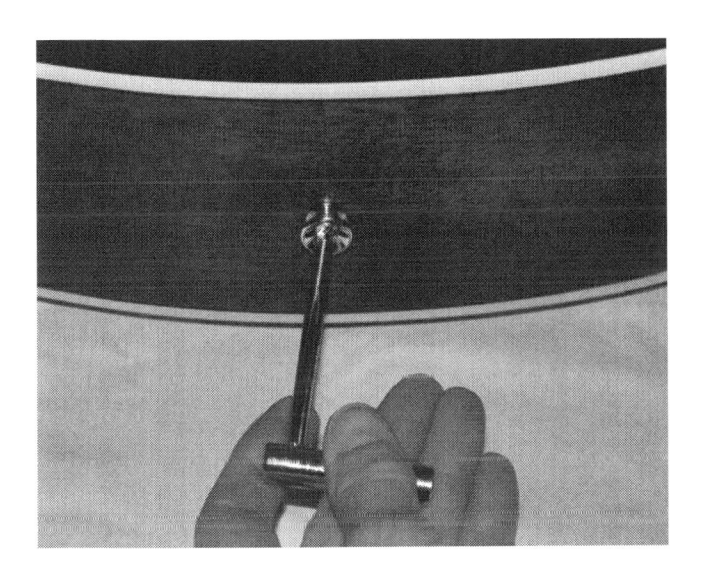

If you have an acoustic/electric guitar you may notice that the input jack has come a little loose. Depending on what kind of input jack you have on your guitar, this can be salved by simply tightening the bold holding the jack. But be careful, there is a proper way to do it and doing it the wrong way can result in breaking the wire connections inside the guitar.

The method shown in the next image is not idea. Using a wrench or socket to tighten the jack will not only turn the nut, but it will rotate the jack inside the guitar causing the wires to twist and come loose. Do this too often and the jack will start to produce static noise or will cut out completely. The best tool for this job is a jack tool. There are a couple of specialty tools on the market, such as the JackTight or the Bullet Guitar Jack Tool. But, if you don't want to invest in a specialty tool that is used maybe once a year, if there is a way you can reach inside the guitar and hold the jack preventing it from turning while you tighten the jack, then you can use a simple wrench.

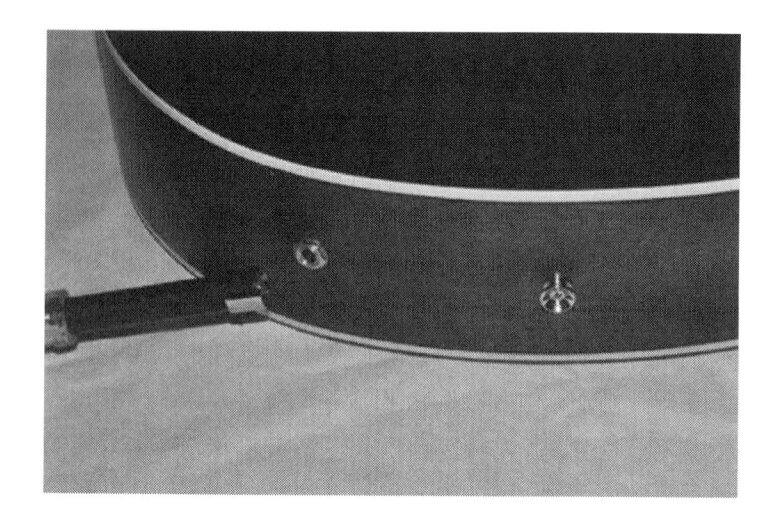

Some input jacks and guitar electronics are easily removable. In the example below, on this Taylor guitar, the input jack and battery compartment are easily removed by taking off two small screws. This allows you to inspect the jack from inside, insuring that the contacts are making a good connection with the cord.

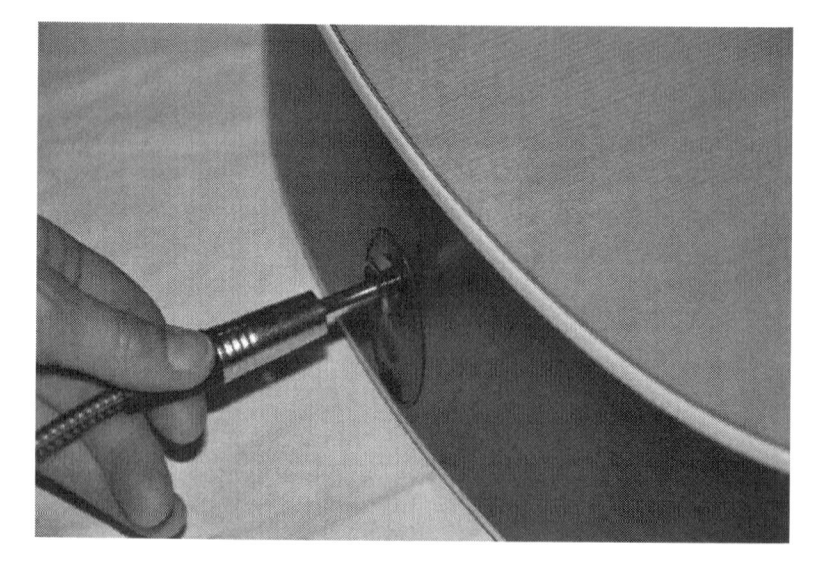

Lastly, you can keep your guitar's electronics in top shape by keeping them clean. Using canned air you can blow out unwanted dust and dirt from control knobs and sliders. Sometimes these electronics are removable as shown in the image below. On this Yamaha it's easy to remove the control unit and remove any dust from the connections or control knobs.

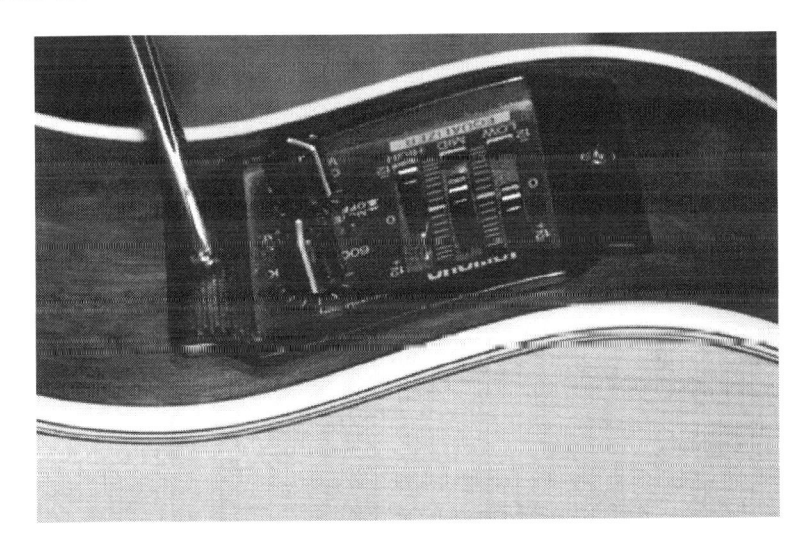

If you are experience unwanted noise,such as a scratchy static noise, when you turn your control knobs or other controls, this can be remidied by spraying a small amount of contact cleaner directly on the knobs. This only works if you have a way to get to the potentiometer they way you would on an electric guitar. But, if you can, spray a small amount of contact cleaning directly into the potentiometer and turn the knob several times to disperse the cleaner. This should take care of any static problems.

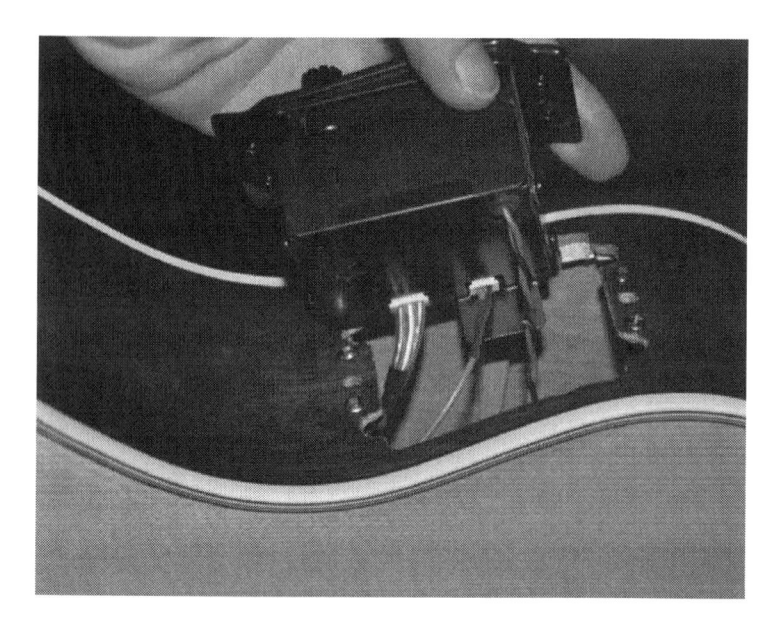

When you take the time to remove parts like this, take a minute to examine the wire connections. Make sure all connectors are securely in place. Make sure all soldering joints are secure and making good contact.

If you are going to experiemnt with taking removable parts off your guitar for cleaning or inspection, always keep track of what you are doing, the order in which you are doing it and any springs, washers, spacer or screws that you remove. When re-assembling anything, work in backwards order from how you took it apart. You should not have left over parts at the end.

Final Words

You may have wondered what happened to the classical guitar from the beginning of this book. The bridge repair was successful. The guitar was placed in a quality hard case with a humidifier for a week. The moisture from the humidifier was absorbed into the guitar body and this helped seal up the large crack in the wood at the top of the guitar.

A new set of strings was installed and, after the strings were allowed to stretch, the truss rod was adjusted. Surprisingly the action on the guitar was very good and the intonation was nearly perfect and did not require adjustment.

That classical guitar went from being a broken, out of tune instrument that sat around hopelessly collecting dust to a decent sounding, functioning instrument that is now being played on a daily basis. The guitar has lost its monitary value, but has not lost its musical value. And that's what it's all about, playing the instrument and making music.

About the Author:

Gayle Monroe has been playing the guitar since her parents gave her first instrument when she was just 10 years old. She has been doing her own guitar maintenance and setup for years on all her guitars and has finally decided to share her experience with others.

We hope you have found this book to be helpful. We hope that you will use the information provided to take good care of your instrument and to keep it in great playing condition. A well maintained guitar is an essential part to a happy and satisfied guitar player. So, take good care of your instrument and keep playing.

She is also the author of another book on this same topic.

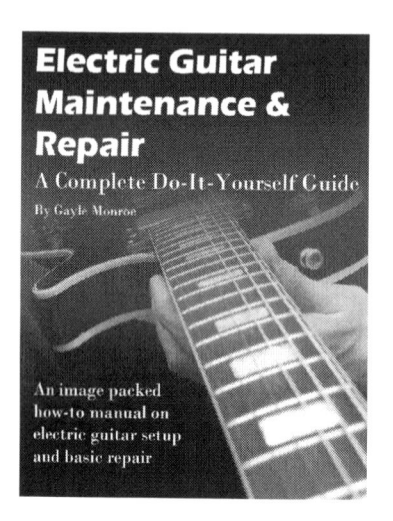

Printed in Great Britain
by Amazon